P9-CCY-174

The EVERYTHING® Girls

100+ ideas for sleepover games, goodies, makeovers, and more!

Ultimate Sleepover Party ♥Book

Laura McIntyre

SEP 1 1 2014

Adams media
Avon, Massachusetts

Publisher Karen Cooper

Managing Editor, Everything® Series Lisa Laing

Copy Chief Casey Ebert

Assistant Production Editor Alex Guarco

Acquisitions Editor Lisa Laing

Senior Development Editor Brett Palana-Shanahan

Everything® Series Cover Designer Erin Alexander

Copyright © 2014 by F+W Media, Inc.
All rights reserved.
This book, or parts thereof, may not be reproduced in any form without permission from the publisher; exceptions are
made for brief excerpts used in published reviews.

An Everything® Series Book.
Everything® and everything.com® are registered trademarks of F+W Media, Inc.

Published by
Adams Media, a division of F+W Media, Inc.
57 Littlefield Street, Avon, MA 02322. U.S.A.
www.adamsmedia.com

ISBN 10: 1-4405-7393-X
ISBN 13: 978-1-4405-7393-4
eISBN 10: 1-4405-7394-8
eISBN 13: 978-1-4405-7394-1

Printed by RR Donnelley, Harrisonburg, VA, U.S.A.

10   9   8   7   6   5   4   3   2   1

June 2014

McIntyre, Laura.
  The everything girls ultimate sleepover party book / Laura McIntyre.
    pages cm.
  ISBN 978-1-4405-7393-4 (pb) -- ISBN 1-4405-7393-X (pb) -- ISBN 978-1-4405-7394-1 (ebook) -- ISBN 1-4405-7394-8
(ebook)
  1. Sleepovers--Juvenile literature. 2. Children's parties--Juvenile literature. I. Title.
  GV1205.M34 2014
  793.2'1--dc23
                          429 8812
    2014010780

Many of the designations used by manufacturers and sellers to distinguish their product are claimed as trademarks. Where
those designations appear in this book and F+W Media, Inc. was aware of a trademark claim, the designations have been
printed with initial capital letters.

Interior illustrations by Kathy Konkle; © iStockphoto.com/McHenry/lineartestpilot/KeithBishop;
© blue67/gollli/Yael Weiss/Alisa Foytik/Len Neighbors/Martina Vaculikova/Olha Sukharevska/Yauheni Kulbei/
Lyudmyla Kharlamova/Marie Nimrichterova/123RF.
Cover images © iStockphoto.com/McHenry; © blue67/123RF.

This book is available at quantity discounts for bulk purchases.
For information, please call 1-800-289-0963.

Contents

Dedication

Dedicated to: My three favorite people in this whole world, my amazing children; **Ashlynn**, **Zoey**, and **Noah**. Thank you for being my inspiration!

Chapter 1

Let's Have a Sleepover Party!

Some call it a sleepover, others a pajama party or slumber party, but the one thing everyone calls it is *fun*! Whether you're celebrating a special occasion like your birthday, or a holiday, or just want to plan a super-fun party with all your closest girlfriends, a sleepover is the best way to have a night (and morning) everyone will remember.

Getting Started

You need to decide on a few major things before you go any farther in planning your party: Who will you invite? When will it be? Should you have a theme? And the one that's probably the most important to your parents: How much will it cost? These are the vital things that you and your parents should talk about *before* you start telling all your friends.

The Guest List

First and most importantly: Who should you invite to your sleepover? Usually, it's a good idea to have no more than 4–8 girls at your party. If you're tempted to invite more, think about it—your friends will be there to see and spend time with you. If you have too many people at your party, it might be hard to pay attention to each one of them, and you might feel overwhelmed. And that is not how you want to feel when you're having a party! This party is about having some serious fun, and making sure that all your guests enjoy themselves. Even though you may want to invite everyone you know (so that you don't hurt anyone's feelings), try to keep your guest list small and manageable so that everyone (including you) can have a good time. If there are friends that you feel bad about leaving out, maybe you can plan to do something with them another time to make up for it.

Pick a Date

Second, you need to pick a date. Before you settle on a date for your shindig, you'll need to check with your parents first to make sure your proposed date is okay with them. They'll probably want to know the basic party plans, like how long your party will last, and if your guests will go home after breakfast the next morning or if you plan to extend the party to include more activities into the afternoon. You'll definitely need to get your parents' permission before you talk to anyone else.

Next, make sure that your friends will be able to come. After all, you don't want to choose a weekend when half your friends will be out of town. Talk to the people you'll be inviting to see if they'll be available on your proposed day. You don't have to fill them in on all your plans, just ask if they'd be around and interested in doing something special with you.

Theme Parties

Does your party need a theme? It's not necessary, but a theme can add that certain something that turns your party from ordinary to extraordinary. A theme party is a great way to share your favorite interests with your friends. If you love baking and trying new recipes, you could have a cooking-themed party. A spa party is great if you and your friends love trying out the latest nail designs or makeup. Do you like to sing and pretend you're a rock star? Are you the queen of gross-out games? Do you love '80s dance music? Check out the theme party ideas in Chapters 3–13 to find one that matches your idea of fun. Or you can take some snippets from one theme and a little from another to create your own unique theme party.

Make a Budget

Next, you'll need to make a party budget. Definitely not the most exciting task, but totally pivotal. How much money can you spend on your party? Again, talk to your parents about what you're planning and make sure they're on board. Creating a budget is a good way to figure out how much everything will cost. Start by making a list of everything you think you'll need for your party. Here are some things to start with:

- Invitations
- Party food and drinks
- Disposable plates, cups, napkins, and utensils
- Decorations
- Games and activities
- Favors for guests
- Breakfast for the next morning
- Thank-you cards

Think of all the things you want to do with your friends during the party and add it to your list. If you plan on going to the movies or ice skating first, add the price of tickets to your list. If you don't plan on having special decorations or favors, you can remove those items. Once you have your list, find out how much each item will cost. For example, will you make or buy invitations? Store-bought invitations are the easiest option, and you can find out how much they cost by visiting a store that sells them or looking online. But if you have art supplies at home, the DIY method can cost almost nothing. (And then you can use that money for other party items!) Talk to your parents about how much food will cost. Think of the games and activities you want to do—do you need any props or prizes? Will you be watching movies? If you don't own the movies, don't forget to add the price of the rental.

Whoa! All that stuff adds up, doesn't it? If your budget seems too high, it's time to go through it again. Look for things you can do without or make yourself instead of buying. You might even be able to borrow some things, like games, decorations, or DVDs. Remember, spending a lot of money on your party doesn't make it special—being a creative party planner is the best way to make sure your friends have a fabulous time!

Sleepover Essentials

Here comes the planning. This is when you'll need to think about the logistics of your party. You might need some parental help to figure out a few of these items, so be sure to discuss the following things with them:

• Who's supervising your sleepover? Most of the other parents will want to know this, and some will want to talk to the chaperone before they give permission for their daughter to attend.

• What will you need for food? Just snacks or dinner? What will you have for breakfast? Do any of your friends have allergies or food restrictions or preferences that your parents need to know about?

- Where will all your friends sleep? Do you have enough space for all of them?
- What are the rules for the party? Do your parents expect everyone to be quiet after a certain hour, or are they okay with giggling and whispering going on late into the night?
- Who will clean up after the party? (It will work in your favor if you offer to help or handle it mostly on your own!)
- What do you expect everyone else in your house to be doing during the sleepover? Are you okay with your siblings interacting with your friends, or would you rather they were kept busy in another part of the house? Do you want a parent to be part of the party, or do you want to be alone with your friends?
- What do your friends need to bring to the sleepover? Unless you have a lot of extra beds in your house, they'll probably need to bring a sleeping bag and pillow. (And pajamas and a change of clothes, of course!) If you want your friends to bring anything else (nail polish, DVDs, music, magazines, or games, for example), remember to let them know on the invitation.

Getting the Word Out

Now that you've chosen the date and decided what kind of party you want to have, it's time to think about your guest's first sneak peek into your party—the invitation. First, you need to make sure you have enough time; you should send the invitations 1–2 weeks in advance of your party.

Now, it's true that you can buy invitations at the store, but creating your own unique invite is a great way to set the tone and get your friends excited for your party. Plus it showcases your many talents! If you're having a theme party, the invitation will also let your guests know what to expect and how to prepare. Each of the theme party chapters later in this book includes instructions for making a fun invitation that focuses on a theme. You can either follow the instructions exactly, or use them as a starting point to come up with your own unique and stellar invite.

Of course, other than being eye candy, the first job of an invitation is to give guests all the information they need about your bash. Make sure your invite includes:

• **Why?** Is it your birthday? Are you celebrating a recent accomplishment? Is it a holiday party? Or "just because"?

• **When?** Don't just include the start date and time. Let your friends know what time they should be picked up from your party as well.

• **Where?** Include the drop-off address as well as any other locations you plan on visiting during the party, like the mall or the movies. Parents will appreciate knowing where their daughters will be throughout the entire event.

• **"RSVP"** stands for a French phrase, *"répondez, s'il vous plaît,"* which means "please reply." Basically, this means you want guests to let you know whether they are coming or not. You could also use "Regrets Only," which means that your friends should only let you know if they are *not* going to be able to make it. Make sure to include a phone number or e-mail address on your invitation. Even if you choose not to ask for an RSVP, parents may want to get in touch with you to ask questions before the event.

Party Food

Parties mean party food! After all, a party is an excuse to have lots of fun, including fun foods that you don't eat every day. And since your party will be going on for a long time, you're going to need lots of food! It's time to make another list—your party grub list. Use this list to plan for your party food, and to make sure you have enough for everyone.

• How many people will you be feeding? Make sure you have enough for everyone.

• How many meals will you have? For most sleepovers, a light supper and breakfast are provided, plus plenty of snacks in between. You'll also need lots of beverages.

• Will your menu be part of your theme? Look for recipe ideas online, or check out the theme chapters for party food to match your celebration.

• Do any of your friends have food allergies? Find out before your party if any of your friends are allergic or sensitive to something, like peanut butter, wheat, or dairy, or if they have other dietary restrictions.

• How long will it take to get everything ready? Make sure you start early enough to have everything prepared or ready to go by the time your guests arrive.

• Do you have everything you need for serving food—platters, plates, cups, napkins, and utensils? Will you use disposable items, or stuff already in your kitchen? Remember, if you don't use disposable plates and cups, someone will have to wash them all!

Deciding on Decorations

Decorating can kick your party up a level and give your space a festive feel. Decorations can range from super simple, like balloons and streamers, to quite elaborate, like a haunted house or a hopping dance club. Your party decorations will depend on your budget and theme, plus your space, taste, and creativity.

You'll find some killer decorating ideas throughout this book. Most of them can even be made at home with just a few simple supplies. There are also lots of ideas for party decorations online. Just search for "DIY party decorations," and you'll be amazed at what you find!

Choosing Games and Activities

Undoubtedly, the greatest thing about a sleepover is getting all your friends together and having as much fun as is humanly possible. You should plan at least three to four activities that you can do throughout the evening. Think about what you and your friends are into. Are you energetic and sporty? Then plan an outdoor game to keep everyone moving. Is everyone into arts and crafts? Visit a crafts store for ideas on something you can all make. (This kind of activity also serves as a party favor. Bonus!)

Activities for a theme party are easy to come up with. See the theme chapters for ideas. Or you can tweak a game or activity so it matches your theme. For example, charades or Mad Libs can be played with '80s clues, or you could have a scavenger hunt with a fashion theme.

Think about whether your friends will prefer cooperative or competitive games. In *competitive* games, you and your friends play against each other. One person or team will be the winner. *Cooperative* games do not usually have winners and losers. They often involve everyone working together to try and reach a certain goal.

Consider how much down time your games will have. Down time is the time other players have to wait to play or take their turns, like games where only one or two players can play the game at a time. Some games that require players to wait their turn are okay, because it's the kind of game where it's fun to watch people take their turn. However, if you choose a game that has a lot of down time and is *not* entertaining for others to watch, you might want to think of another activity your friends can be doing while waiting their turn.

Chapter 2

The Traditional Sleepover

The most popular type of sleepover (because it is awesome!) is a traditional slumber party: hanging out with your best friends, eating all your favorite foods, laughing and playing games until all hours, and continuing the party at breakfast. All you need for this all-night funfest are sleeping bags, munchies, a few games or movies, and, of course, friends. Here are some ideas to make your traditional sleepover legendary.

Eye Mask Invitations

These cute eye mask invitations are a unique way to invite your friends to your sleepover!

What You Need

8.5" × 11" white card stock (1 sheet for every 2 invitations you want to make)
Pencil
Scissors
Pens or fine-tip markers
8.5" × 11" fun patterned paper (1 sheet for every 2 invitations you want to make)

Glue gun
Glue
Rickrack trim (1 28"-long strip per invite)
Single-hole punch
Ribbon (1 24"-long piece per invitation)

How to Make

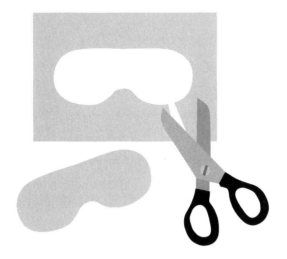

1. Draw and cut out an eye mask shape onto white card stock. The mask should be approximately 6.5" wide by 3" tall (you should be able to fit two on one sheet of card stock).

2. Use this shape as a template to trace as many eye masks from the white card stock as you need. *Don't* cut them out yet. Using a pen or fine-tip markers, write your party details on each eye mask.

4. Cut out the sleep masks.

3. Glue the patterned paper onto the reverse side (the side without writing) of the card stock. Let dry.

6. Punch a hole at either side of the eye mask. Thread a piece of ribbon through one hole, then the other. Tie a knot at either end of the ribbon.

5. Starting at the nose part of the mask, use your mini glue gun to attach the rickrack around the entire mask. Work in small sections, gluing about every inch or so apart, so that the rickrack stays in place.

Menu

The traditional sleepover menu includes lots of awesome grub—pizza, chips and dip, popcorn, cookies, brownies, and candy. You know what you and your friends like; just make sure you have enough to last you all night! If you like to make special treats, here are some easy-to-make recipes for party munchies.

Mix and Match Snacks

Homemade snack mix is a fun treat to make before a movie marathon. Set out bowls of mini pretzels, mini marshmallows, dried fruit, chocolate chips, M&M's, peanuts, and different cereals. Give each of your friends her own bowl or bag to create a personalized snack mix.

Fruit Kebabs

Set out a selection of bite-sized fruit: strawberries, pineapple chunks, kiwi slices, grapes, apple cubes, or melon balls. Provide skewers for your friends to create their own fruit kebab. Vanilla or fruit-flavored yogurt makes a great dip to serve alongside the skewers.

Tie-Dye Cupcakes

What could be cooler than cupcakes with a swirl of colors inside?

What You Need

Vanilla cake mix
Food coloring (4 colors)
Cupcake wrappers
Cupcake pan
Prepared vanilla cake frosting

How to Make

1. Prepare vanilla cake mix according to directions on box.

2. Divide the batter into four separate bowls. Make each bowl a different color by stirring in 2–3 drops of one of the food colorings to each bowl.

3. Place the cupcake wrappers in the cupcake pan.

4. Spoon the colored batter into the cupcake wrappers randomly so that there are spoonfuls of different batters in the same wrapper. Don't stir the batter, simply give one gentle swirl of a toothpick.

5. Bake according to cupcake directions on box. Cool cupcakes on a wire rack.

6. Frost cupcakes with vanilla frosting.

Rainbow Pancakes

Here's a fun idea for breakfast in the morning. Mix up your favorite pancake batter and divide it into separate bowls. Add different food coloring to each bowl and cook separately to create a rainbow of different colored pancakes. Want to get even more creative? Add chopped fruit to the colored batter before cooking. Try strawberries in red batter, blueberries in blue batter, and bananas in yellow batter.

Decorations

Before you start to decorate, make sure your party area is clean. There's nothing grosser than a guest finding old food on the floor or an old Band-Aid under the couch, yuck! So the first step is to remove any junk, sweep or vacuum the floors, and clean the bathroom. When decorating, you can either go big or small, depending on your budget and how much time you have. Either way can be fabulous; it's all in what you make of it. Here are just a few DIY decorating ideas you could try.

• **Fill your space with balloons.** If you have a color scheme for your party, choose those colors, or use all the colors of the rainbow. Helium balloons are fun, but you can also tie ribbons to air-filled balloons and tape them to the ceiling.

- **Create a fun banner** to welcome your friends to the party. You can use poster board or a roll of art paper. Make it colorful and festive. Include all their names, and pictures of all the fun things you'll be doing together.

- **Create a collage** on the wall with pictures of you and your friends. If you've known each other for a long time, be sure to include pictures of everyone in younger days.

- Use markers, poster board, and scissors to **draw and cut out giant images of fun sleepover items** like pajamas, nail polish, slippers, sleep masks, makeup, music, pizza, or anything else you can think of. Hang the pictures on walls throughout your party area.

- **Use your snacks and treats as part of the decor.** Set out festive bowls or decorated jars full of candy.

- **White lights** strung across the ceiling make wonderful "stars" to sleep under with your friends.

- **Don't forget music!** Decorating isn't just about what you see—it involves all your senses. You can just have the radio playing in the background, or you can take the extra step and create a playlist beforehand featuring your favorite songs.

- **Turn your dining table into a "bed."** Make a headboard using cardboard and paint. Use tablecloths, but place them on the table as you would sheets and blanket on the bed. Place a small pillow or two next to the headboard to complete the effect. Now place the table settings or buffet on the "bed" to create a fun, whimsical feasting area for your friends.

Games

The best party games are easy to learn, fast-moving, and laugh-out-loud funny! Here are some games everyone will love.

No-Peek Obstacle Course

Set up a simple obstacle course that your friends will try to make it through . . . blindfolded!

What You Need

An obstacle course built from soft things such as pillows, cushions, blankets, or stuffed animals. (Remember, players will be blindfolded as they make their way through it, so you don't want to use anything in your obstacle course that they could hurt themselves on.)

Blindfold

Flag to be placed at the end of the course (if you don't have an actual flag, that's okay; the flag can be anything from a small stuffed animal to a comb)

Timer

Pencil and paper

How to Play

1. Divide players into teams of two. Each team decides which one of them will be blindfolded. The other one will be the guide.

2. One team goes at a time. The blindfolded player takes her place at the beginning of the obstacle course. Start the timer and say, "Go!"

3. The blindfolded player must find her way through the obstacle course as her teammate guides her, using only her voice. At the end of the course, the blindfolded player must find and grab the flag.

4. Once the blindfolded player grabs the flag, stop the timer and mark down how long it took for that team to make it through the course.

5. Let all of the teams get a try at the obstacle course. The team with the best time wins!

Foot Volleyball

This slumber party game is a blast! Who would guess that you could play volleyball indoors? Instead of a volleyball, you use a balloon, and instead of hands, you must use your feet!

What You Need

A large open space

Volleyball net (or piece of rope or string)

Balloon

How to Play

1. Set up the net so that the top is only about four feet off the ground. If you don't have a net, you can stretch string or rope across the middle of the playing area.

2. Have all the girls remove their shoes and divide them into teams.

3. The teams take their sides of the net, and everyone lies on her back.

4. One player starts the game by serving—throwing the balloon up over the net. Using only your feet, continue playing as if you were playing regular volleyball. No one may use her hands during the game, except for serving.

5. Score just like you would for regular volleyball.

Sock Wrestling

This is a hilariously fun game. Two people face each other on a carpeted floor on their hands and knees. Both players wear socks, but no shoes. The first person to remove both of the other person's socks wins! It's so simple, but *so* much fun.

Pucker Up

Can you and your friends identify each other's lip puckers?

What You Need

White napkins or sheets of paper

Lipstick

How to Play

1. Give every player a sheet of white paper or napkin.

2. Have everyone slather on the lipstick (the same shade) and make five different kissing prints on their sheet. Don't show anyone.

3. Mix up all the pages and display them for everyone to see. Everyone must try to guess whose lip prints belong to whose lips. The one who guesses the most correctly wins!

Taste the Rainbow Race

The hardest part of this game is trying to do it without laughing!

What You Need

Big bowl of Skittles   *Straws*   *Cups*

How to Play

1. Have everyone sit in a circle and give each player a straw.

2. Place the bowl of Skittles in the middle of the circle, and place a cup behind each player.

3. On the count of 3, players must try and move as many Skittles as they can into their cups by sucking them onto their straws and transporting them to their cups without dropping them.

4. When the big bowl is empty, count up the number of candies in each player's cup. The one with the most Skittles is the official winner, but everyone gets to keep and eat their Skittles afterward!

Guess Whose Secret!

Can you and your friends guess whose secret is whose?

What You Need

Index cards   *Pens*   *Large bowl*

How to Play

1. Give each player three index cards and have her write a secret or fact about herself that no one in the room knows. It's a good idea to try to disguise your handwriting so your friends won't recognize it.

2. Players then fold their cards in half and place them in a bowl.

3. Take turns pulling out a secret and reading it to the group. Let everyone take a guess as to whose secret it is.

4. After everyone has made their guess, the secret keeper can confess it was her secret . . . or not.

Activities

Not all fun has to be in game form of course. Activities are a great way to bond with your friends and have fun. Activities can be anything your friends and you like to do together. The following are some traditional sleepover activities that you might like to try.

Tents

Provide sheets, blankets, cushions, and pillows. Clothespins and yarn are also great to have handy when you're going for ultimate tent construction. Enlist your friends to help build a massive tent for you all to sleep under, or let each girl build her own personal tent.

Movies

Movies are a great end-of-the-night activity. Rent or borrow a few movies, and make sure there is variety. A good rule of thumb is to choose something scary, something funny, something romantic, something new, and one of your classic favorites that you've seen a thousand times. When it's time for the movie, let your friends know the choices and then put it to a vote.

Note: To avoid making any of your friends afraid or uncomfortable, take the scary movie out of the vote if anyone has a real fear of them. It's not cool to tease or torture a friend like that. We all have fears; consider how you would feel if your friends used yours against you.

Makeover

Sleepovers are known for the girliest of all girly things . . . the makeover! Invite your friends to bring their makeup, hair products, nail polish, and other beauty products, and give each other makeovers.

Favors

Friendship pillowcases are classic sleepover favors. Every time one of your guests uses the pillowcase, she'll remember all the fun she had at your party!

What You Need
A white or light-colored pillowcase for each guest and yourself
Large alphabet stencils

Fabric paint
Fabric markers

How to Make
1. Before the sleepover, use the fabric paint and stencils to personalize each pillowcase with a guest's name. Let dry completely.

2. At the sleepover, give out the personalized pillowcases and let your friends use the fabric markers to write fun messages and notes on each other's pillowcases.

3. Other sleepover favor ideas:

• Nail polishes with custom labels

• A framed picture of all of your friends huddled together in your PJs. You could even make this one of your party activities. Buy craft frames at your local craft store (one for each friend). Provide paint, stickers, sequins, glue, fabric, and so on, and let your friends each design their own friendship frame.

• Friendship bracelets

• A goodie bag full of candy

Chapter 3

Spa Party Sleepover

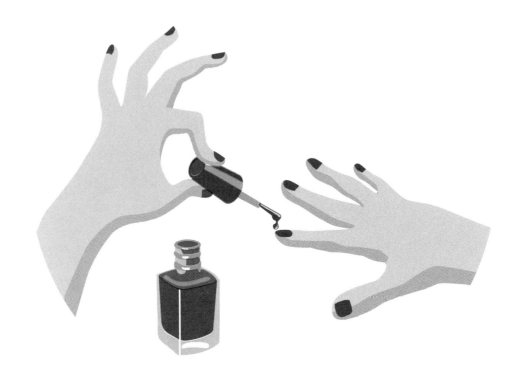

Get your friends together for a deluxe pampering spa party! You'll all have a blast making homemade beauty supplies, giving each other manicures and pedicures, and noshing on some spectacularly delicious treats. Of course, you'll have loads of laughs with some pretty funny games and activities. Just beware—all the moms might want to join in your girlfriend fun!

Nail Polish Invitations

Invite your friends to your sleepover SPArty with a unique invitation in the shape of a nail polish bottle.

What You Need

Glitter construction paper in your choice of colors
(1 standard 8" x 11" sheet for each invitation)
Scissors
Glue
White card stock
Black card stock
Craft sticks (one for each invitation)
Fine-point markers or gel pens in different colors

How to Make

1. Fold a sheet of glitter paper in half horizontally, with the glitter on the outside.

2. Cut the sides off the folded paper as shown to form the shape of a nail polish bottle. The top opening needs to be at least 3 inches wide.

3. Squeeze a line of glue along the outside edges, leaving the top opening unglued.

4. Cut out a piece of white card stock 3 inches wide by 5 inches long. Write your party details on this with pen or marker. Cut a 3-inch by 3½-inch rectangle from the black card stock.

5. Glue the white rectangle to the bottom of the craft stick and the black rectangle to the top of it, as shown here. Doesn't it look like the nail polish cap and brush? Let dry for about 15 minutes.

6. Insert the white rectangle into the opening on the top of the nail polish bottle shape. Leave the black part outside the opening.

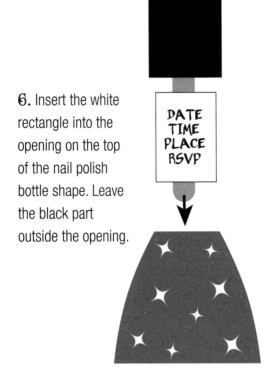

7. Cut an oval shape from white card stock to create a label for the front of the invitation. Glue it to the front of the nail polish bottle invitation.

Spa Menu

For a luxurious spa feel, set out platters of fruit, colorful veggies and dips, and finger sandwiches for delicious light snacks. Create big pitchers of "spa water" by adding thin slices of lemon and cucumber, mint leaves, and strawberry slices to a pitcher of ice water.

Offer some fun and fancy foods that your friends don't get to eat every day, or present ordinary food in an extraordinary way. Here are a few ideas to get your creativity flowing.

Marshmallow Manicure Treats

They look like little nail polish bottles, but they taste like sweet deliciousness. Create these fun treats using marshmallows and miniature Tootsie Rolls. Before you get started, line a baking sheet with paper towels and set a cooling rack on top of the paper towels.

Mix a few drops of food coloring with about a tablespoon of water in a small saucer. Use a few different colors for variety. Roll the marshmallows in the tinted water, then place them on the rack to dry. Unwrap a Tootsie Roll and push it into the top of a marshmallow.

Finger Sandwiches

Finger sandwiches have a way of making you feel fancy. Make sandwiches using thinly sliced bread. Use whatever you like for fillings—cucumber and hummus, turkey and cheese, peanut butter and jelly, or chicken salad. Use cookie cutters in pretty shapes—flowers, hearts, stars—to make spa-tastic sandwiches. Set the different shapes on cute plates, and use your best handwriting to make little signs describing what's inside. Garnish the plates with frilly lettuce leaves, sliced fruit, cherry tomatoes, or tiny gherkin pickles.

Chocolate-Covered Strawberries

Fruit and chocolate are quintessential spa yummies. Have an adult help you melt your favorite chocolate in the microwave and dip delicious, ripe, red strawberries into the melted goodness. Place each covered strawberry into its own mini cupcake wrapper. To help chocolate firm up and to make sure the treat stays fresh, keep these refrigerated until party time.

Frozen Chocolate Kiwi Pops

These healthy pops are pretty and scrumptious! Line a baking sheet with parchment paper. Peel ripe kiwi fruits and cut them into thick slices. (You'll probably get three or four slices from each kiwi.) Ask an adult to help you melt a bowl of chocolate morsels in the microwave. Insert a lollipop stick in the side of each slice and dip it into melted chocolate until it's completely covered. Place on parchment paper and freeze. They'll be ready to eat in 2–3 hours.

Pinkie Pie Punch

This gorgeous pink punch will be the hit of the party! Check out your local party store for festive plastic glasses to serve this sweet and fizzy drink.

1 (46-ounce) can of pineapple juice
2½ cups of water
1 (6-ounce) can of frozen pink lemonade concentrate, partially thawed
1 quart of berry sherbet, softened
3 (28-ounce) bottles of ginger ale

Pour pineapple juice and water into a large punch bowl. Add lemonade concentrate and sherbet, and mix well. Stir in ginger ale and serve immediately.

Decorations

For a spa party, you want a setting of beauty and relaxation—hello, just like a spa! Turn on some relaxing music or nature sounds, and light some scented candles. A bunch or two of supermarket flowers can be split up among many small glasses and bottles throughout your "spa." Put beauty supplies in cute baskets and decorated boxes. Roll up towels and make a pyramid of them. When your guests arrive, you want them to feel instantly relaxed.

Here are some decorating ideas to turn your party space into a calming and soothing retreat.

• Create tissue paper flowers and hang them from the ceiling, or create bouquets and display them in simple glass vases around your party area.

• Use a calligraphy font to create signs for different stations at the party, like "Manicures" and "Make Your Own Lip Gloss." Print your signs on colored or glittery paper. If you have some extra photo frames, you can frame the signs to make them look more special.

• Find some pictures online of nail art or makeup application tips you'd like to try. Print these out and hang them at the appropriate station.

• Purchase clear ornament balls from your local craft store. Use fishing line to hang them at different lengths from the ceiling to create a floating bubbles effect.

• Fairy lights are a great way to add special ambience to the room. String them along the walls, across the ceiling, or along a staircase. An entire string of battery-operated mini lights inside a glass bowl or vase makes a glittery centerpiece. Just make sure all electric cords are tucked out of the way.

• Simple bowls filled with smooth river rocks make tranquil centerpieces.

• Use a variety of glass vases or bowls to hold your beauty items, like cotton balls, bath salts, cotton swabs, or sliced cucumbers.

Games

In between spa treatments, make some time for these fun and creative games.

Guess That Scent

Challenge your friends' senses of smell in this battle of the scent-ses!

What You Need

A scarf or a bandana you can use as a blindfold

A collection of things that have a scent—the more scents, the better (Try essential oils, bananas, strawberries, lemons, oranges, coffee, chocolate, cinnamon, vanilla extract, pepper, or toothpaste.)

Paper lunch bags

Marker

Paper and pen

How to Play

1. Before the guests arrive, place each item in a separate bag and label the bag with a unique number using the marker. Close the top of the bag.

2. On the paper, write each guest's name across the top, and the numbers corresponding to the bags down the left side. This chart will be used to record the players' guesses.

3. Blindfold one player and present her with one of the bags. Open the top of the bag, hold it under her nose, and tell her to inhale deeply. Ask the player to guess what's in the bag. Record her guess on the chart.

4. Repeat with all the other bags.

5. After everyone has had a turn, reveal all the items and announce who correctly identified the most scents. She is the victor!

Nail Art Contest

Pull out the nail polish and let your friends compete for the best nail art.

What You Need

Acrylic nails

Nail polish—as many different colors as you can find

Small detail brushes or nail art pens

Toothpicks

Foam makeup sponges

Nail glitter

How to Play

Give each player three acrylic nails and allow 30 minutes for players to create their masterpieces. Present all the nail art to an impartial judge to award prizes for most creative, most detailed, or most colorful. If an impartial judge is unavailable let each girl secretly score each nail from 1–5 in each category (5 being the best). Add the scores up and present the top 3 scores for each category to your friends. You do not need to share all scores. No one needs to have their feelings hurt by knowing they came in last.

Smoothie Contest

Many spas offer healthy juices, herbal teas, and yummy smoothies to their patrons. Let your guests compete to make the most colorful and tasty smoothie! Check with a parent to find out if they want to supervise this activity.

What You Need

Frozen or fresh fruit, like strawberries, blueberries, bananas, pineapple, apples, or peaches

Spinach or kale

Orange or other fruit juices

Milk or yogurt

Peanut butter or almond butter

Ice cubes

A good blender

Cups or glasses

How to Play

Set out all your ingredients and challenge your friends to come up with a delicious smoothie using whichever ingredients they choose. Let everyone try each other's finished concoctions. You can vote for the "best" or just trade recipes.

Guess Which Celebrity

Can you and your friends recognize your favorite celebrities by their eyes alone? How about just by their nose, or mouth?

What You Need

Celebrity magazines
Scissors
Pens and paper
Index cards
Glue

How to Play

1. Before the party cut out several large photos of easily recognized celebrities. Assign each celebrity a letter. On a sheet of paper, write down the names and corresponding letters.

2. Cut each photo into strips, showing only eyes, nose, or mouths. Glue each strip onto an index card and mark the back of the index card with the correct letter assigned to that celebrity.

3. Mix up all the index cards and lay them all out face-up on a table. Give each player a pen and paper to write down what parts she thinks belong to which celebrity. To make the game a bit easier you can provide a list of celebrities for the players to choose from.

4. Once all players have finished their guesses, check them against your list. The girl with the most correct answers wins!

Activities

Let the pampering begin! You and your friends can try out lots of different beauty treatments, and you can even make your own beauty supplies.

Fruity Lip Balm

Create your own lip-smacking, fruity lip balm with a few simple ingredients. Make them all one flavor, or experiment with different drink mixes for a variety of colors. You can find little plastic containers for the gloss at a beauty supply store, or search for "lip balm containers" online. You will need an adult to help you with this project.

What You Need

1 cup petroleum jelly (such as Vaseline)
Flavored and sweetened drink powder (such as cherry, grape, strawberry, or fruit punch)
Lip gloss containers

How to Make

1. In a medium-sized bowl, microwave petroleum jelly for 3 minutes, stopping every 30 seconds and stirring well. Stop when the petroleum jelly is completely liquefied. Be careful—it will be *very* hot. Use oven mitts to remove the bowl from the microwave.

2. Carefully stir the drink powder in, a spoonful at a time, until you're happy with the color. Stir well until all the powder is dissolved. If the petroleum jelly starts to harden or thicken too much while you're mixing, heat it in the microwave for another 30 seconds.

3. With an adult's help, carefully transfer your mixture into your lip gloss containers and leave to harden for at least 2 hours.

4. If you want to make different flavors, divide the petroleum jelly into smaller microwave-safe bowls and add different drink powders to each bowl.

Oatmeal, Milk, and Honey Facial Mask

A facial mask is a lovely, relaxing way to take care of your skin. This mask is perfect for sensitive, acne-prone, and dry skin. It will leave your face feeling heavenly. The recipe will make enough for four facial masks.

What You Need

2 cups uncooked oatmeal (not instant)
2 cups water
2 cups milk
Hairbands and/or ponytail elastics
4 tablespoons pure honey
8 thin cucumber slices, chilled
Washcloth and warm water

How to Make

1. Pour oatmeal, water, and milk in a large saucepan. Stir well to combine.

2. With an adult's help, heat the oatmeal mixture over medium heat for 10 minutes. Stir the mixture frequently as it heats. Remove the pan from heat and let the mixture cool for 15 minutes.

3. Have your guests pull their hair back from their faces with a hairband or ponytail holder, and lie down in a comfortable place. On clean, dry skin, massage a tablespoon of honey over each girl's face, avoiding the eye area.

4. Apply the oatmeal mask over the honey, using upward strokes. Avoid the eye area. Place a cucumber slice over each eye. Let your guests lie quietly for 10–15 minutes.

5. Remove cucumber slices. Gently rinse the mask off with a soft washcloth soaked in warm water.

Manicures

A manicure is a fabulous way to pamper your friends. And every time they look at their beautifully groomed nails, they'll remember the fun they had at your party. Perhaps some moms or older sisters could volunteer to give everyone manicures. Or you can split up into pairs, and take turns being a manicurist. Be creative; try different colors of polish or nail stickers to create unique nail designs. Here's a step-by-step guide to the perfect manicure.

What You Need

Hand towels

Exfoliating scrub, or a mixture of ½ cup sugar and 1 teaspoon liquid soap

Cotton balls

Nail polish remover

Bowl of warm water mixed with 1 teaspoon of liquid soap

Emery boards

Cuticle softener

Cuticle pusher

Moisturizing lotion

Base coat

Nail polish

Hand lotion

Step-by-Step Manicure Guide

1. Set up a manicure station. Spread out a clean towel on a table or tray, and lay out all your supplies on it.

2. Gently massage the exfoliating scrub all over the hands of the friend receiving the manicure to remove any dead and flaking skin. Wash and dry hands.

3. Remove any old nail polish using cotton balls and nail polish remover.

4. Using gentle strokes, file the nails down to create a smooth, even shape.

5. Massage cuticle softener into each nail bed and into the cuticles, then soak hands in the bowl of soapy water for 5 minutes.

6. Very gently, push back cuticles with the cuticle pusher. Afterward wash and dry their hands.

7. Apply one coat of base coat. Let dry for 5 minutes, then apply two coats of polish, with dry time in between each coat. Let nails dry completely—at least 15 minutes.

8. Finally, massage their hands with the hand lotion.

Spa Favor Kit

Send each of your friends home with a spa-to-go kit. You can use a bath caddy, a cute tote bag, or perhaps even a small tub (big enough to soak your feet in) as the container. Get creative with the contents! Here are some ideas for what to include:

- Scented hand or body lotion
- Facial scrub
- Nail polish
- Flip-flops
- Manicure set
- Cotton balls

- Loofah sponge or a nylon puff
- Beauty magazine
- Shampoo and conditioner
- Body wash
- Eye mask
- Chocolate bar

Chapter 4

Fashion Fest Sleepover

Have you and your friends ever dreamed of being fashion designers and creating your own one-of-a-kind looks? If you and your friends are aspiring fashionistas or fashion designers, this could be the perfect theme for your sleepover. With these party theme ideas, exploring your fashion sense has never been more fun!

Stiletto Invitation

There are tons of pre-made invitations you can purchase for this theme. But if you love fashion, then you probably love to design, so why not use that creativity and design your own invite? Follow these simple instructions to create a fabulous shoe invitation.

What You Need

8½" x 11" black card stock (or preferred color; 1 sheet for every 2 guests)
Scissors
White unlined paper

Markers
Ribbon
Access to a color copier (if possible)

How to Make

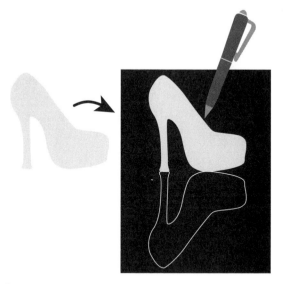

1. Draw and cut out a basic outline of a stiletto shoe on half a piece of card stock. This is your shoe template.

2. Trace it onto the upper half of another piece of card stock. Flip your template and trace another shoe upside-down directly under the first shoe, making sure to line up the heels and stiletto bottoms so that they are slightly overlapping.

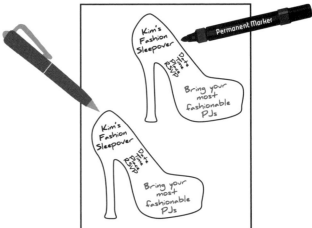

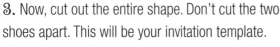

3. Now, cut out the entire shape. Don't cut the two shoes apart. This will be your invitation template.

4. Use the double shoe template to trace and cut out as many invitations as you are going to need. Fold each in half to create a stiletto card.

5. Now you need to create an insert to write your party details on. Use your first cutout (the one with the single shoe) and trace it onto the upper half of a plain white piece of paper. You should be able to fit two on a page.

6. Write all of your party details inside the shoe shape.

7. Photocopy as many of these as you need. Insert one copy into each stiletto invitation. If you don't have access to a copier, handwrite the details for each invitation.

8. Once you have all the invitations assembled, hole punch the top corner of the creation. Make sure the hole goes through all three pieces of paper.

9. String a ribbon through the hole and secure with a bow. Voilà! Your invitations are ready to be passed out to your fashion-minded friends!

Fashionista Menu

It's time to create your fashionable feast! Let your creativity and design skills go wild as you invent delicious and stylish treats. Here are some fabulous fashion-related menu items to give you some ideas.

Pizzazz Popcorn

Add some pizzazz to popcorn by coloring it a fashionable color such as pink, purple, or whatever your favorite color is. Have an adult help you make this treat on the stove.

What You Need

2 tablespoons butter
2 tablespoons vegetable oil
½ cup corn syrup
½ teaspoon of your desired food coloring
⅔ cup popcorn kernels

How to Make

1. Simply combine butter, oil, corn syrup, salt if desired, and food coloring in a bowl with popcorn kernels.

2. Place mixture into a large pot. The mixture should form a single layer on the bottom.

3. Cover pot with lid.

4. Turn the stovetop to medium-high heat.

5. Gently swirl the pot over the heat. After a few minutes the popcorn should start to pop. (Ask an adult to help with this step to avoid getting burned with hot oil!) Watch carefully so that it doesn't burn. When pops get more than three seconds apart, you are ready to take it off the burner.

6. Spoon colored popcorn onto wax paper and let cool. The mixture you cooked it in will create a yummy, crunchy coating. After it cools, store it in a zip-top bag.

More Menu Ideas

- **Paparazzi Pizza:** Before the party, prepare pizza dough in the shape of a simple dress. You want to make these small enough so that each girl can have her own pizza. Provide plenty of toppings so that guests can "design" their own fashion pizza creation.
- **Fashion Cookies:** You can purchase cookie cutters in the shape of shoes, purses, and other fashion items. Bake up some cookies in these shapes and decorate them with assorted frosting and sprinkles; better yet, let your guests decorate their own. Another idea is to use the cookie cutters on sandwiches to create fashionable finger food.
- **Fabulous Cups:** No ordinary cups will do for your fashion diva friends. Serve drinks in disposable plastic martini glasses. You can also use these to hold candy or nuts at your buffet table. You can pick these up at most local party stores.

Consider using brightly colored or zebra print trays and bowls to make any food you serve appear more fashion friendly.

Decorations

Okay, time to set the stage! Here are some fashionable DIY ideas that'll have your guests walking into your party and feel like they are on a fashion show runway.

- Purchase a roll of basic red fabric and create a red carpet for your guests to walk down. This would be perfect for an easy-to-do runway.
- Purchase sheets of poster board and cut out silhouettes of fashion models as large as you can make them. If you want them closer to life-size, you can use three sheets of poster board in the same color. Line them all up top to bottom and draw your silhouette over them using one for the top half, one for the middle, and the last for the bottom half of your model. Hold the three pieces together using transparent

tape on the back. Make as many as you would like in different poses and hang them on the wall in your main party room.

• Spread brightly colored and zebra or other animal print tablecloths on your buffet or dining table. Look for cutlery, tableware, and balloons in these prints, too.

• Remember that decorations create ambience, and ambience is important for your ears as well as your eyes. Create a fun playlist before your party with high-energy tracks and hard-hitting beats.

• Create your own fashion magazine! Use a graphics program to create a fashion magazine cover. Create magazine titles and headlines, and place the words over a fashionable picture of you. You can make multiple covers using different pictures of your friends. Pick up a couple of your favorite magazines to get ideas. You can then have these printed at your local print shop, and hang them up around your party room. You could even go big, and have them printed poster size.

Games

This is the part where you and your friends get to dive into the fashion world with some fabulous games! So break out that imagination and harness that creative spark, because these games are sure to put your fashion sense to the test!

Name the Era!

This is a great game to play to test your friends' knowledge of fashion history. You can set this up for them to play when they first arrive at the party.

What You Need

Three different pictures of fashion from each decade from the '50s until now (You can easily find these on the Internet.)

Marker

Piece of paper and pen for each player

How to Play

1. Print out all the fashion pictures. Note down which one comes from which year on a master reference sheet for yourself.

2. Cut each picture out and glue them onto a poster.

3. Number each picture. Write that number next to each image on your poster with a marker.

4. When your friends arrive, challenge them to try and guess which decade each fashion item came from. Provide each person with a piece of paper and pen to write their guesses on.

5. After everyone has handed in their answers, add up who had the most correct guesses. She is the winner!

Fashion Magazine Scavenger Hunt

In this game, you and your friends must divide into teams and scour through fashion magazines as quickly as you can to find specific fashion items you will use to make a fashion collage.

What You Need

Several fashion magazines (Start collecting these a few weeks before your party; ask friends and neighbors for their old ones.)

1 sheet of poster board for each team

1 pair of scissors for each player

1 bottle of glue or glue stick for each team

1 copy of the scavenger hunt list for each team (see next page)

Timer

How to Play

1. Divide players into teams of two or three.

2. Provide each team with a sheet of poster board, scissors, glue, at least 3 fashion magazines, and the scavenger hunt list (see following).

3. Set the timer for 30 minutes.

4. On "go," players must search through their magazines to find the different items on their list. Once they find an item on their list, they must cut it out and glue it to their team's poster board collage. Each item can only be counted once per team.

5. When time runs out, whichever team has glued the most items from the list onto their collage wins!

You can create your own list or use this one:

- Tiara
- Lipstick
- Perfume bottle
- Green high-heeled shoes
- Boots
- A pair of red lips
- Tie
- Wedding dress
- Polka-dot top
- Any animal print article or clothing or accessory

- Runway
- Sunglasses
- Purse
- Wild hairstyle
- Sequined article of clothing
- Red dress
- Diamond gemstones
- Flower in hair
- Hat
- Designer nails

Fashion Designers

See if you have what it takes to create a fashion "masterpiece"!

What You Need

Tissue paper
Newspaper
Trash bags
Aluminum foil

Items to help attach the materials (clothespins, string, tape, safety pins, etc.)
Ask your friends to bring other materials— anything except actual fabric!

How to Play

1. Divide your friends into two or more teams.

2. Give each team the same materials.

3. Each team picks a model from their group.

4. Each team gets 20 minutes to dress their model using only those materials.

5. When the time is up, the models show off their outfits by walking the runway.

6. Either vote, or have a impartial judge decide who is:

- Best dressed
- Most creative
- Weirdest or wildest

Come up with your own categories, and have a blast!

Fashion Pictionary

In this game, you and your friends take turns drawing outfits that someone would wear for different occasions. One person draws, and the others have to try to guess when or where someone would wear that outfit.

What You Need

Paper   *Pen*

Colored pencils or markers   *Bowl*

How to Play

1. To prepare for the game before the party, you will need to write different occasions on individual slips of paper, fold them up, and place them all in a bowl. You can have your parents do this, if you would like to play as well. Ideas for occasions may be:

- Something you wear to the beach
- Something you wear on a date
- Something you wear to get married
- Something you wear to go to work
- Something you wear to sleep
- Something you wear to a ball or dance

2. Divide players into two teams.

3. The first team chooses a person to draw. That person pulls a folded paper with an occasion written on it out of the bowl. No one else can see what she picked.

4. That person has 1 minute to draw an outfit and have the other team guess what occasion it is for. The person cannot draw words or speak them.

5. If the team guesses correctly, then they get the point for that round. If they do not, then the other team gets one guess to try and steal their point. If no one guesses correctly, neither team gets the point.

6. It is now the next team's turn.

7. Keep playing, letting everyone have a turn at drawing. You can play as many rounds as you want, as long as each team has an equal number of turns.

8. The team with the most points at the end of the game wins!

Ooh LaLa!

Activities

This is where your creativity can come out to play. There are tons of activities you and your fashion-minded friends can conjure up, but here are a few fun ideas:

• Purchase a variety of fabric remnants from your local fabric store. Pull out your old Barbie dolls and use them as models. Use the fabric, along with scissors and fabric glue, to see who can create the coolest outfit for their model.

• Make your own jewelry! Accessories definitely can make or break an outfit. Set up different stations for you and your friends to design and create your own one-of-a-kind jewelry. You can purchase ready-made kits, or you can purchase individual jewelry-making supplies at your local craft store. Spice it up and have one station for earrings, another for necklaces, and another for bracelets. Your friends can make them for themselves, or everyone can make them and then trade.

• No fashion party slumber party would be complete without a makeover! Have all your friends bring their makeup, hair products, hair accessories, and nail polish. Team up and give each other beauty makeovers. Have everyone share her favorite beauty secret.

Fashion Favors

Personalized Sketchbooks

A fun and creative favor for your friends to take home with them is a personalized design sketchbook that they can keep all their designs in. Personalize the cover and add some drawing tools, and you will have created a favor that is memorable and useful!

What You Need

A sketchbook for each guest

A sketch pencil or set of colored pencils for each guest

Adhesive printing paper

Access to a computer graphics program and printer with a scanning function

Ribbon

How to Create

1. Measure the cover of your purchased sketchbooks.

2. On a blank sheet of paper, draw a box the size you would like your personalized cover to be. You will want your covers to be at least an inch smaller all the way around then the actual sketchbook cover.

3. Write "Fashion Sketchbook" in large letters. You can also include a personalized message in smaller letters underneath, such as "Sarah's 12th Birthday 2014."

4. Now it's time to get creative! Use your markers to design your fashion cover any way you like. You might want to draw some fashion models or sketches, or you might want to use some fashion pictures you printed from online, or cut out from magazines. How you decorate your cover is completely up to you.

5. You now need to scan your image and have it printed in color on the adhesive paper. Print one cover for each scrapbook.

6. The adhesive paper acts as a giant sticker. Peel the back of each cover and attach it to the sketchbooks.

7. Optionally, you could glue little individual accents to each cover, such as sequins, bows, glitter, etc. You could even write each girl's name on her book, to add an extra personalized touch.

8. Place the colored pencils on top of the finished sketchbooks and secure them together with the ribbon.

9. Give one to each friend before they leave the party as a thank-you for attending your bash.

Rock Star Sleepover

Time to rock and roll all night! Who wouldn't want to be a rock star? With the cool ideas for this rockin' party, you and your friends will feel like real music icons. You'll glam it up in true rock star fashion, and enjoy music-themed snacks and games that will keep you roaring with laughter and rocking to the beat all night long!

Concert Ticket Invitations

VIPs only! You need a ticket to get into this superstar soiree! Make your invites look like tickets to the best show in town. You can either use a graphics program on your computer and then print out the number of copies you need, or you can design your own unique invitations by hand. The one shown here is just one example—you can also find lots of other samples online to inspire you. Once you've finished creating your invitations, place them in envelopes and throw in a bit of confetti. That way when your guests open their invites they'll get a fun surprise and a small hint of what awaits them at your rockin' party!

Musical Menu

You'll need to eat if you're going to be jamming all night long! Here are some cool ideas to coordinate your menu plans with your rock star theme.

Microphone Treats

These treats not only look fabulous . . . they're delicious!

What You Need

Pre-made crispy rice treats (either bought in a box or made ahead of time by you)
Sugar cones
Chocolate candy wafers
Chocolate sprinkles

How to Make

1. If packaged, unwrap pre-made rice cereal marshmallow treats. Shape rice cereal treats into a ball.
2. Melt chocolate candy wafers in microwave, according to the package instructions.
3. Dip each cereal ball into melted chocolate, then place the coated ball on top of the sugar cone.
4. Before the chocolate hardens on the ball, cover it with chocolate sprinkles.
5. Place in airtight container and store in a cool, dry place until party time.

Star Cookies

You can have your own Hollywood star with these cookies! Use your favorite sugar cookie recipe and a large star cookie cutter to make cookies shaped like stars. Get creative with the frosting, and label each cookie with your friends' initials or names. You can really make your star cookies shine by using metallic sprinkles in gold and silver.

Rock Star Cupcakes

Turn regular cupcakes into fun tributes to your favorite singers.

What You Need

Cupcakes (already baked, frosted, and ready to eat)
Full body pictures of your favorite rock star idols (you can print these from your computer or cut them out of magazines)
Heavy card stock in bright colors
Glue
Invisible tape
Toothpicks or craft sticks

How to Make

1. Glue your rock star pictures onto card stock.
2. Cut out the image, leaving a small outline of the card around the body.
3. Attach a toothpick or craft stick to the back side of the card stock.
4. Insert the toothpick into the top of your cupcakes. Voilà!

Celebrity Menu Items

It's easy to turn any menu item into a rock star–themed buffet by getting creative with the names. Rename your entrées after your favorite artists by creating tent cards for each dish. To create a tent card, all you need to do is fold a 4" x 6" piece of card stock in half and write the food's reimagined name on it. For added pizzazz, glam the cards up with glitter and stickers. Try these names:

- Katy Perry Party Dip
- Maroon 5 Munchies
- Lady Gaga Guacamole
- Aguilera's Awesome Appetizers
- Beyoncé Berry Muffins

Other Diva Snack Ideas

- Pop Rock candy
- Rock candy in assorted colors
- Popcorn (Pop-Star Corn)

Decorations

To decorate your pop star party, you will want to bring on the glitz and glam. Here are some ideas to spice up your party scene:

- Purchase old records from your local thrift store. Even scratched ones will be fine, and would probably be really cheap. You can use the records in multiple ways: as decorative mats for your table settings, hung on the walls, as food trays, etc. You can even spray paint them bright, fun colors.
- Cut out stars from poster board. Cover them with glue, and sprinkle on some gold or silver glitter. Hang the stars throughout your party area, on the walls or from the ceiling.
- Hang white string lights throughout the party, or around other decorations.
- Cut musical notes out of black construction paper and hang them on the walls.
- Display feather boas of assorted colors, along with hats, sunglasses, and other diva fashion objects throughout your party area.
- Cover balloons with silver glitter and hang from the ceiling with string.

Games

Who is the coolest of them all? Here are some rockin' game ideas that will let your friends compete to see who is the smoothest and coolest rock star.

I'm a Rock Star?

Friends are all given a rock star identity; the only problem is that they don't know what that identity is. It's their job to figure it out!

1. When your friends arrive at your party, tape an index card with the name of a famous singer written on it on their back.

2. Your friends can see everyone else's identities, but they cannot look at or be told who is written on their card.

3. The object of the game is for your friends to try and figure out what singer they each are by asking the others "yes" or "no" questions about their identity.

4. The first player to correctly guess her own identity wins!

Don't Forget the Lyrics!

In this fun, action-packed game, your friends will get to dance and groove to the music, but when it stops one of them will be on the spot to complete the lyrics.

1. Before the party you will need to create 15–20 slips of paper, each with a different lyric from a song. Each lyric should have a few words missing.

Example: "Hey, I just met you, and this is crazy, but here's my number ＿＿＿ ＿＿＿ ＿＿＿ ＿＿＿."

2. Next, place each slip into its own balloon. Inflate the balloon and knot the neck. Place all the balloons into a trash bag until you are ready to start the game.

3. When you are ready to play, designate someone to start and stop the music at random intervals. Ask a parent or an older sibling to help out so everyone can play!

4. Pull out one balloon and tell your friends they must bop the balloon to each other while the music is playing.

5. When the music stops, whoever was last to touch the balloon must pop it, then try to fill in the missing lyrics written on the slip inside. If she gets it correct, she can stay in the game; if she gets it wrong, she is out.

6. Continue playing until there is only one player left. She is the winner! If you would like to make the game shorter, just use two or three balloons for each round.

Songwriting Competition

This is a hilarious game that you and your friends can play if you have a karaoke machine.

What You Need

Karaoke machine

A variety of well-known songs for the karaoke machine in a playlist

Timer

Paper slips and pens

How to Play

1. Divide players into groups of two or three.

2. Let each one choose a song from your karaoke playlist.

3. Put 25 minutes on the timer. During that time, teams must come up with new lyrics for the songs.

4. When the time is up, teams can each perform their new song. Everyone can vote for the best by writing their choice on a slip of paper. Whoever gets the most votes wins!

Who Sang It?

Which of your friends knows their music the best?

How to Play

1. Before your party, make a list of 10–12 famous singers or bands. For each of the singers, you will also need to make a list of 10 of their songs, listed from least known to most popular.

2. When you are ready to play, divide your friends into two teams.

3. The object of the game is to identify the artist of each song. Read the list of song titles one at a time, starting from the least popular. Each team gets one guess after each song is called out.

4. The first team to guess the artist correctly gets the points. However many songs are left on that artist's list after the correct answer is called is the number of points that team gets.

5. Continue playing until you have gone through all the artists. The team with the most points wins!

Boa Limbo!

The limbo is always a party hit. Instead of a limbo stick, use a feather boa and see how low your friends can go!

What You Need

Feather boa
Limbo music

How to Play

1. Have two people hold the boa, each holding one end at chest level, stretched out between them.

2. Start the music. You and your friends line up, and each player takes a turn shimmying under the feather boa to the music. You can lean backward, but not forward, and the only thing that can touch the ground is your feet. If someone falls or breaks any of the other rules, she is out.

3. After you and your friends have each had a turn, the boa holders lower the boa by about six inches, to about waist height. Everyone can then go another round. After each round, the boa is held lower and lower until all but one of the players have fallen out. The last player standing is crowned Limbo Queen!

Activities

- **Diva Makeovers:** Have all your friends bring their makeup and other diva props. Provide fun costumes and accessories such as hats, boas, jewelry, etc. Help each other glam up, and take plenty of pictures during and after.

- **Rock Out:** After you and your friends are dressed to the nines, it's time for the show. Have your karaoke machine set up and let your friends pick their favorite songs to perform.

- **Make a Video:** Do you and your friends have a favorite song? Work together and make a music video. Have fun setting up scenes, singing, and using your collective creativity to make a fan music video for your chosen song. Check out YouTube for inspiration.

• **Pose for the Paparazzi:** Take turns being the paparazzi, and snap tons of pictures of each other. To add a creative spin on them, have your friends pose for different fun headlines, like, "Red Carpet Beautiful," "Caught Red-Handed," and "The Secret She's Not Telling."

Swag Bag Favors

At many big celebrity events, swag bags are given out to the guests. These bags are often filled with promotional items and merchandise. You can make your own swag bags for your friends filled with fun rock star products.

What You Need

A small canvas bag for each guest (you can find these at your local craft store)
Glue
Fabric markers
Decorative embellishments of your choice, such as glitter or sequins
Swag to put inside (see following)

How to Make

1. Use the craft supplies to give each swag bag a glitz and glam makeover. You can write each guest's name on her bag to add a personalized touch.

2. After you are done creating your bags, it is time to fill them with the swag. You can choose whatever you would like to fill your swag bags with. Here's a list of some fun stuff you can put inside:

- Lip gloss
- Nail polish
- Hair accessories

- Glitter lotion
- Makeup
- Bath soap

Chapter 6

Super Fan Sleepover

Do you have a favorite celebrity? Maybe you are a huge fan of a certain musician, band, actor, author, book series, movie, or TV series. Whatever it is that you're a fan of, you can create a super-fun party theme for it! You'll need all your creative juices flowing and plenty of prep work beforehand, but the following ideas will help you climb the pinnacle of fandom and make your party the envy of any super fan!

Super Fan Invitations

The invitation is a great opportunity to get creative and show off your fandom! A collage invitation is one idea to get the word out on your fan girl theme.

Collage Invitation

One fun way to create an invitation is make a collage using pictures and images of your theme. If, for example, you are a fan of the band One Direction, you could cut out images of the band and individual pictures of the members, and arrange them on a piece of card stock. You can find images in magazines or the Internet. If you're a fan of a certain book or book series, you can print out memorable quotes from that book to create your collage. You could even draw images and use your own fan art to create a collage! Once you complete your collage, it is time to add the party details. You can display these on your collage any way that you like; the most important thing is that they are easily visible and readable. One way to do this is to write the details on another piece of card stock (you can use different colors, if you like), cut out the individual words, and paste them onto your collage. Once you have completed your collage, you can take it to a local print shop and print out color copies of the invitation to hand out to your friends.

Creative Phrasing

Maybe your chosen theme lends itself to an invitation idea on its own merit. An example of this would be if you were a fan of the Hunger Games book and movie series. Your invitation can use the theme and wording from the series to creatively invite your friends to the party. For example, a girl named Hannah was celebrating her thirteenth birthday and she used the following wording for her Hunger Games invitation:

Your name has been drawn in the Panem Reaping
You are hereby required to report to the Capitol to participate in

Hannah's 13th
Hunger Games
Birthday Sleepover

Date: August 14–15
Arena Location: 1234 Mockingjay Lane
Tribute Drop-Off Time: Friday 5:00 p.m.
Survival Pick-Up Time: Saturday 11:00 a.m.
May the odds be ever in your favor

Think about your theme. If it's a book or movie is there any way to incorporate the ideas or events that happened in the story into your invitation?

Iconic Symbols

Another creative idea is to design an object invitation that relates to your theme. For example, if you were doing a Harry Potter theme, you could purchase small owl plush animals. Write all your party details on a piece of parchment and roll it up like a scroll. Attach the scrolls to the owls, and deliver them to your friends.

Other object invitations could be:

• Favorite Band or Musician: A toy microphone (you can purchase or make them) with the party details inside
• Cinderella: Send the invitation inside a plastic "glass" slipper.
• *Vampire Diaries* or *Twilight*: Write your invitation in fake blood and attach it to a set of plastic vampire teeth.

Fabulous Fan Food

Sometimes a theme will naturally lend itself to a certain menu; other times you'll need to get a little creative. Here are some ideas to tie whatever you're a fan of to some kind of food theme:

• If your theme is a band, find out what each member's favorite foods are and serve those at your party. You can create labels for each item. For example, if you are having a One Direction theme sleepover, you could serve one of Zayn's favorite dishes, spicy chicken pasta, and have the label identifying it read "Zayn's Fave Pasta."

• Another idea is to use word play. This way, you can serve whatever menu items you would like and just come up with a fun label for it to tie it into your theme. For example, if you are having a Harry Potter sleepover, you could serve mac and cheese and label it "Magical Macaroni." Other dishes might be "Dumbledore's Dumplings," "Slytherin Surprise," or "Hogwarts Hoagies."

• If your theme is a movie, you can use foods seen in the movie to serve at your party. For example, you could serve "Peeta's Bread" at a Hunger Games party, or serve jellybeans at your Harry Potter party and call them "Bertie Bott's Every Flavor Beans."

Decorations

Decorating your party space in homage to your favorite thing is a must for any super fan. Show how strong your love is by plastering your theme all over your party. Here are some ideas to help you get started:

• **Speech bubbles:** Cut white poster board into the shape of speech or thought bubbles, and use a black marker to write quotes from your theme on them. Post these around your party area, or use them as props in photos of you and your friends.

- **Posters:** Maybe you have a movie poster from your favorite film, or a group shot of your favorite band. If you have posters, they are an obvious and easy decorating item. Plus, there's nothing so cool as seeing your favorite thing large and in charge all over your walls.
- **Slideshow:** Create a slideshow on your computer using pics and/or clips from the object of your fandom. Add music to it, and set it up to play during your party.

Sample Decorating Ideas

Here are some examples of what other super fan girls did to decorate their parties.

Natalie was a huge fan of the Hunger Games series. She used objects and ideas from the movie to decorate for her Hunger Games slumber party. She created little parachutes to hang from the ceiling, and attached objects like bread, containers, and bottles marked "medicine" and "water." She purchased toy arrows and displayed them in glass vases around her party area. She also hung a banner that read "May the Odds Be Ever In Your Favor," along with a huge mockingjay cutout she had created.

Lara threw an awesome One Direction bash for her twelfth birthday. She created a huge wall collage using posters of One Direction that she had collected. She chose the colors of the British flag as her color scheme, using dark red, blue, and white for her balloons, streamers, and table settings. For her centerpiece, she used a cutout of the number 1 and the letter D. She also cut out about a dozen hearts from red poster board, and wrote lyrics from her favorite One Direction songs on them. She hung these on the walls throughout her party space.

Zoey was crazy over the young heartthrob country artist Hunter Hayes. For her party, she purchased a large cardboard standup of Hunter to greet her visitors. She created two large H's out of cardboard boxes that she covered in giftwrap with a heart pattern. She also used small red and black balloons to create a wall collage. She taped red balloons on the wall to create a giant heart, and in the middle of the heart she created a giant H out of black balloons, filling in the rest of the heart with more red balloons.

Games

Coming up with games that center around the object of your fandom can seem hard at first, but here are a few game ideas that you can use with almost any theme.

Plant the Kiss

This game takes the classic birthday game of Pin the Tail on the Donkey and gives it a new twist.

What You Need
A poster of your celebrity crush   *Lipstick*
Blindfold   *Pen*

How to Play
1. Hang the poster on a wall with plenty of open space around it.
2. Have all your friends put on a thick layer of lipstick.
3. One at a time, blindfold each friend, and spin her around three times.
4. Point her toward the poster and let go. Without peeking, their goal is to kiss the poster and leave their lipstick print as close to the celebrity's lips as they can. Once each person takes their turn, write their name next to their print.
5. The player whose lips land closest to the lips on the poster wins!

Body Parts Identifier

Can you and your friends identify the object of your fandom by their eyes alone? How about their nose, lips, or hairline?

What You Need

Magazine cutouts or Internet printouts featuring headshots of the celebrity of your choice

Magazine cutouts or Internet printouts of other celebrity headshots

Scissors

Index cards

Glue

Paper and pencils

How to Play

1. Cut the individual features out of each headshot (such as the eyes, nose, lips, chin, hairline, ears, and so on).

2. Glue them to individual index cards. Number each index card, and on a separate piece of paper mark which celebrity each number belongs to.

3. When you are ready to play the game, spread the prepared index cards out on the table and provide each of your friends a pen and paper.

4. Challenge them to identify which index cards belong to the star celebrity of the evening.

5. Whoever identifies the most correct body parts wins!

Fill in the Blank

A great game to test out your friend's fan knowledge!

What You Need

Index cards

Pen

How to Play

1. Before your party, write a different lyric or quote from your theme with a word missing on each card. If your theme is a musician or band, use lyrics. If your theme is a book or movie, use quotes. If your theme is a celebrity you can either use quotes or facts about the celebrity.

2. You will need to create 25–50 fill-in-the-blank clue cards.

3. When you are ready to play, divide the players into two teams.

4. You play the game host, and start by reading a fill-in-the-blank clue. The first team to call out the correct answer wins the card.

5. If both the teams call out the correct answer at the same time, then the players that called out the answer must have a thumb war to see who wins the card.

6. Whichever team has collected the most cards by the end of the game wins!

ABC Scavenger Hunt

Divide your friends into teams and challenge them to search the house or neighborhood to find items that relate to your fan theme. The challenge is to collect one item for each letter of the alphabet. Provide a time and place where everyone must meet back up and present what they have found. Let each team explain why each of their items relates to the theme, and have an impartial judge (like a parent or a sibling) ready to give the items a thumbs up or thumbs down. For every thumbs up, the team receives a point. The team with the most points wins!

Activities

Activities at your super fan party should involve the object of your fandom, of course. So if your theme is a movie, watch the movie. If it is a celebrity, watch a movie that they star in. If it is a band or musician, dance like crazy to their music. Other ideas for activities could include:

- **Fan Art:** Provide paper, pencils, markers, and other art supplies to your friends and let them express their fandom through art.
- **Cover Songs:** If your theme is a musician or band, pull out the karaoke machine and let everyone perform their favorite song.

Fan Fiction Contest

Can you and your friends create a new story for the characters of your favorite book or movie?

What You Need

Index cards   *Imagination!*

Pen

How to Play

1. Before the party, write individual words on each index card. This could be a random phrase, object, person, place, as well as words that are associated with the theme somehow. Fold each card in half, so the word is not showing. You can have your friends help you with this part, so that the words come from everyone.

2. Sit in a circle with your friends. Choose one person to start a story using the characters of your theme. She must first draw a card and use that word as part of her story.

3. Going clockwise around the circle, the next person draws a new card and continues the story the first person started, making sure to incorporate the new word or phrase in the story. She can add a few sentences to the story, or a few paragraphs. When she is finished, she passes the story on to the next person.

Super Fan Favors

Your favors should definitely be related to your fan theme. Here are just a few ideas you could create for your friends that will unite you all in true fan girl fashion.

- A T-shirt for each girl with quotes from the book or movie, or lyrics if your party is music related.
- A charm bracelet with different charms related to your theme.
- A special treat or item related to your theme.
- A goodie bag filled with small items that all relate to the theme.

Chapter 7

Food Fest Sleepover

Are you culinary chic? This party theme is full of deliciously fun party ideas for you and your girls to explore the arts of cooking, baking, and eating. From the decorations to the games, everything in this sleepover is centered around the art of food. This party is full of creative yumminess—the ultimate theme for any food lover!

Recipe Card Invitations

Set the tone for your culinary bash by creating super-cute and ultra-creative recipe cards! But not a boring old recipe card . . . you're going to spice things up! Your sleepover announcement goes where the name of the recipe is usually found, and the details of your big event are put where you'd normally see the ingredients and directions.

You can create your invitations by hand with paper, pen, and markers, or on the computer using a graphics program. You can use the following sample as inspiration. Once you complete your recipe card invitation, copy and print enough for all your friends, and get the word out!

Food Fun Menu

At a food party, the main focus of the event is going to be the food, of course! Working out your menu is the main decision that you will need to make, as this will influence the kind of decorations and activities that you'll plan. The following ideas include a pizza party, a cookie party, and a fondue party, but you can do whatever you like!

Pizza Party

See who can come up with the craziest and tastiest pizza! You will need to go on a big grocery store run beforehand. Stock up on a wide variety of pizza toppings so you'll have everything (and anything!) your guests might need. You can find recipes online to make your own dough, or you can purchase a bunch of prepackaged mini pizza bases so that all you will have to do is decorate and cook. But whatever you do, don't just stick to the typical pepperoni, cheese, and sausage!

What You Need

Here are some suggestions to get your pizza creativity bubbling:

Pizza crust (prepackaged is easiest, or you can make your own)
Chopped veggies (peppers, spinach, broccoli, avocadoes, onions, tomatoes, mushrooms, olives)
Meats (sliced pepperoni, sausage, chicken, bacon, hot dogs)
Chopped fruits (strawberries, pineapples, blueberries, cherries; pie toppings work well)
Cheese (Mozzarella, Provolone, Cheddar, Parmesan)
Sauces (pizza sauce, marinara, barbecue, cheese sauce, ranch, hot sauce)

Have a contest with your friends to see who can come up with the most original pizza. Have a taste contest, with everyone voting on her favorite, or just make as many different kinds of pizzas as you can think of, then feast on them all!

Cookie Party

Do you have a sweet tooth? Invite your friends over for a cookie creation celebration. Pick out a few of your go-to recipes, or get some basic ingredients and try creating your own best-cookie-ever recipe. Either test your recipe beforehand, or be daring and go for some unexpected (but hopefully not inedible!) results at your party. Be sure to write down all the steps, in case you ever want to re-create the recipe again. Here is a fabulous recipe for the best-ever chocolate chip cookies to get you started.

Best-Ever Chocolate Chip Cookies
Yields: 2 dozen cookies

Ingredients

2 sticks of real butter

1 cup white sugar

1 cup brown sugar

2 eggs

2 teaspoons vanilla

¼ teaspoon sea salt

1 teaspoon baking soda

2 teaspoons hot water

3 cups flour

2½ cups semi-sweet chocolate chips

1. Preheat oven to 350°F. In a large bowl, mix together butter, white sugar, and brown sugar. Next add eggs, vanilla, and salt.

2. In a small bowl, dissolve the baking soda into the hot water, then blend into the butter/sugar mix. Mix in the flour and the chocolate chips.

3. Spoon out the cookie dough in small balls, about 1 inch around. Place on an ungreased cookie pan about 1 inch apart. Bake for 12 minutes.

4. Take out of the oven and place on parchment paper. Let cool. Enjoy!

Fondue Party

So many things taste better dipped in chocolate or cheese! If your family has a fondue set, it's time to pull it out, and get dipping! Have an adult show you how to safely use the fondue set if you're not familiar with it. You can decide beforehand whether you would like to melt cheese or chocolate, or you can choose both if you have two fondue pots. The best part about a fondue fest is all the food you can dip. The more variety, the better! Here are a few suggestions:

Chocolate Fondue

Fruits such as strawberries, sliced apples,
diced pineapples, and banana slices
Marshmallows
Brownie bites
Chocolate sandwich cookies
Angel food cake

Cheese Fondue

Chunks of French bread
Sliced sausages
Cherry tomatoes
Chopped broccoli
Shrimp

Note: Fondue is lots of fun, but always make sure there's an adult present to supervise the use of the fondue set, and make sure to have a fire extinguisher on hand as well, just in case. Safety first!

Decorations

Here are a few ideas to set the mood for food, fun, and feasting!

1. Purchase balloons and paper chef hats. Inflate each balloon and tie a string or ribbon to the knot. Cut a small hole in the top of the chef hat and pull the string through it so that the balloon is wearing the hat. Use tape to secure the hat in place on the balloon. Attach the end of string to the ceiling. Create as many of these as you want! You and your friends can have fun adding faces to the balloon chefs.

2. Create large pictures of your favorite foods using posterboard and construction paper to hang on your walls. After all, who doesn't love giant cookie art? Yum-o!

3. Pin a plain apron on the wall (you can get these at craft stores), and have your friends sign it in fabric paints and nonwashable markers (also available at craft stores). The apron can then double as an awesome keepsake.

4. To make a fun banner, cut out a dozen or more 8" circles using posterboard (you can use a dinner plate as a template). Cut out pictures of your favorite foods or food-related words from magazines, then glue the pictures onto the circles, creating mini collages. String the circles together, and hang them in your party area.

Games

Challenge your friends to one or all of these fun food-themed games!

Food Face-Off

You need at least four people to play this game. Divide your friends into two teams. Each team is presented with an identical set of ingredients. During a predetermined amount of time, each team must create a dish using only the ingredients provided. The teams don't have to use all the ingredients, but they cannot use anything additional. It's best to make this a no-bake contest, so that you don't have any problems with using or sharing an oven. The best-tasting dish wins!

Recipe Scavenger Hunt

This game will take some preparation and creativity, but if you are up for the challenge, it's a blast!

What You Need

A printed copy of a yummy recipe with 8–10 ingredients that you know your friends would love to make and eat!

All the ingredients for your chosen recipe (These do not have to be premeasured. A clue leading to flour can just lead to a bag of flour. Just make sure you have enough of the ingredients to complete the recipe!)

Pen and paper or index cards to write your scavenger-hunt clues on

How to Play

Hide your ingredients around the house, or outdoors. Create a clue for where your friends can find each ingredient, writing the clues on a piece of paper or index card. They'll all need to work together, following one clue to the next, to collect all the ingredients for the recipe. It's most fun if each clue is set up to be solved in a different way. Here are some examples of different clues you can create.

INGREDIENT	CLUE
Flour	*A picture of a flower*
Peanut Butter	*The next clue rhymes with "tree hut clutter"*
Vanilla Extract	*Unscramble the letters NLAAVIL TTXCREA*
Sugar	*Pictures that start with each letter in the word "sugar"*

For the last clue in the table above, here is an example: sun, umbrella, ghost, apple, rat. Line them all up in order on an index card. You could add a message, such as "To solve this clue, you gotta be smart, and the answer is found at each picture's start."

The final clue needs to be the recipe itself. You can hide it anywhere, as long as you come up with a clue that will lead your friends there. For example, you could hide the recipe behind a wall clock (a lightweight one that will not break if taken down or moved), and have the clue read:

I have a face that does not smile or frown,
I have no mouth, but I make a familiar sound.
I have hands, but fingers I do not.
I don't walk, but I move around a lot.

Hiding Your Clues

The first clue will not be hidden, but will be given to your friends at the start of the scavenger hunt. This clue will lead to the first ingredient, and the next clue. When hiding your clues, remember that one clue must always lead to the next, until the final clue is found. For example, you would not hide the flour riddle in the flour; you would hide it with the ingredient found just before it, so that it will lead players to the flour next. The clue hidden in the flour should then lead them to their next clue, and so on.

After the Scavenger Hunt Is Finished

After your friends have found and collected all the ingredients and the recipe, it's time for the grand prize! What is the grand prize? It's getting to make and eat the recipe, of course. Yum!

Taste Test

Did you know that over 70 percent of your taste comes from your sense of smell? Your sense of taste only allows you to make a distinction between sour, sweet, bitter, and salty. Let's see how well your friends can taste when they can neither see nor smell the food they are eating!

What You Need

Pudding cups of five different flavors (chocolate, vanilla, banana, lemon, and butterscotch)
Blindfold
A cotton ball for each player
A spoon for each player

How to Play

1. Choose one of your friends to go first.

2. Have her tear her cotton ball in two pieces, and use them to block her nostrils so she can't smell.

3. Blindfold her and make sure she can't see.

4. Feed her a small bite from each pudding cup. After each taste, let her guess which flavor she thinks it is.

5. Write down her guess, and what the actual flavor is.

6. Mix up the order of the flavors, and then give your next friend the same test. When all your guests have taken the test, let them give it to you. When everyone has had a turn, see who identified the most flavors correctly!

Other Activities

Here are some fun culinary-themed activities for you and your friends. Bon appétit!

Decorate Aprons

Why not send each of your friends home with an apron that they decorated themselves? So cool! This is a good activity for the beginning of the party, because once you've decorated your own aprons, you can use them for your other activities.

What You Need

Plain white apron for each of your friends (these are available at craft stores)
Fabric paint and nonwashable markers (also available at craft stores)

Give each of your friends an apron, and have each one decorate hers to represent her taste and style! When everyone's finished and the paint is all dry, you can model your aprons for each other.

Watch a Food Movie

After you and your friends have cleaned up the kitchen, brushed your teeth, and put on your pajamas for the night, you still won't want to go to sleep! (Aren't sleepovers for staying up late?) A movie is the perfect thing to incorporate at this point in your party. If you are looking for the perfect food movie, consider one of the following:

- *Ratatouille*
- *Cloudy with a Chance of Meatballs*
- *Willy Wonka and the Chocolate Factory*
- *Cupcake Wars* (this is a TV show, not a movie, but still a great series)

Friendship Cookbook

Create a friendship cookbook that includes all your friends' favorite recipes!

What You Need

Scanner

Printer

Paper

Yarn or ribbon

Three-hole punch

8½" × 11" card stock, or sheets of posterboard (enough for each friend to have a front cover and a back cover)

Scissors

Pens, markers, and/or paints

How to Make

1. Before the party, invite all your friends to bring their favorite recipe(s) to the sleepover.

2. Collect all the recipes, then scan and print each one. You will need to print enough of each recipe so that you have one for each of your friends and yourself.

3. Pass out one copy of each recipe to each of your friends.

4. To make the cookbook covers, either use card stock, or have your friends cut two rectangles from a sheet of posterboard. The rectangles should be just slightly bigger than the recipe pages.

5. Place all the recipes between the two cover rectangles, and make sure the pages are all lined up together along the left edge, top, and bottom. Then punch three holes down the left side of the book, through all of the covers and all of the pages.

6. String ribbon or yarn through each hole, and secure all three sets of holes. Knot the ends of the string at the edge of the book. Let your friends decorate the covers!

Favors

What better favor for a sleepover than to send your friends home with something they can bake in their own kitchens? Prepare these layered cookie mixes before your party, so that they're ready to be passed out when everyone goes home.

What You Need

1 glass storage jar for each of your friends

All of the dry ingredients in the recipe—flour, brown sugar, salt, baking soda, candy-coated milk chocolate pieces (such as M&M's), white sugar—enough to make as many jars as you need

A printed or handwritten copy of the following recipe (to attach to each glass storage jar)

String or ribbon

How to Make

1. Clean and dry all the glass storage jars well.

2. Place 1¼ cups flour into the bottom of each glass storage jar.

3. On top of the flour layer, add ½ cup of packed brown sugar.

4. On top of the brown sugar, layer 1 teaspoon of salt and 1 teaspoon of baking soda.

5. On top of the salt and baking soda, layer ¼ cup of candy-coated chocolate pieces.

6. On top of the candy-coated chocolate pieces, layer ¼ cup of white sugar.

7. Secure lid on jar.

8. Write out the following recipe onto an index card–sized piece of paper. Leave enough room at the top of the recipe card to punch a hole. Copy and print enough for each glass storage jar that you are making.

9. Punch a hole in the top of each recipe card, and string a ribbon through it. Tie the ribbon around each glass storage jar.

10. Present to your friends!

Mmmm Mmmm Good Cookies

Yields: 1 dozen cookies

Ingredients

1 stick of softened butter
1 egg
¾ teaspoon vanilla extract
Contents of this jar

1. Preheat oven to 350°F.

2. In a large bowl, combine softened butter, egg, and vanilla extract.

3. Add contents of recipe jar, and mix well!

4. Chill the dough in the refrigerator for 5–10 minutes.

5. Drop dough by spoonfuls onto cookie sheet (about 1 inch in diameter, and placed 2 inches apart).

6. Bake for 9–11 minutes.

7. Let cool, and enjoy!

Chapter 8

Totally '80s Sleepover!

Like, no way! It's a total blast from the past with this 1980s-themed sleepover bash. Grab your neon hair accessories and your leg warmers, and get ready to party! You and your friends will bring back the fun and fashion of the '80s all night long. So take a chill pill or gag me with a spoon, this party is going to be totally tubular!

Cassette Invitations

One totally awesome way to bring the '80s back is to make these retro cassette-tape invitations.

What You Need

Blank cassette tapes (with blank labels) for each invitation you would like to make (You can still easily get these at office-supply stores and online.)
Colored markers

How to Make

Simply write your party information on the cassette tapes, and pass them out to your friends. For added fun, if you have a cassette recorder available, you could record a couple of your favorite '80s songs on the tapes before handing them out.

Rubik's Cube Invitations

The Rubik's Cube was a very popular three-dimensional puzzle in the '80s, and it makes a fun invitation! Rubik's Cubes are still widely available today, so you may have seen one, or you may even own one. A Rubik's Cube is a plastic, hand-held cube made up of multicolored squares on each side. When you first buy it, all of the squares on each side of the cube are of the same color. Once you twist and turn the cube to mix all the colored squares up, the challenge is to get the colors back to their original sides, with all the squares on a side being of the same color.

What You Need

A 3" × 3" Rubik's Cube for each invitation you would like to make (Do not mix up the sides of the cubes!)

1" × 3" colored adhesive labels that match the colors of the Rubik's Cube

Craft knife, such as an X-acto knife (If you've never used one of these, get an experienced adult to help you—craft knives are very sharp!)

Colored markers

How to Make

1. Cut the adhesive labels to fit over the squares of the Rubik's Cube. The easiest way to do this is to place a label over a row of its coordinating color on the Rubik's Cube, then use the craft knife to cut the label to fit over each individual square. Do this until you've covered each side of the cube.

2. Use your markers to write a different detail of the sleepover on each side of the cube. For example, write the date on the red side, the time on the green side, the location on the yellow side, and so on.

3. It's best to hand out this fun invitation already "solved." You *can* choose to twist the Rubik's Cube a couple of times, challenging your friends to get the details of your party by solving it. However, it's not recommended, unless you know you're giving it to a friend who can do it!

Gnarly '80s Decorations

Here's a fun way to make a Rubik's Cube for an awesome decoration for your party!

What You Need

A square box or boxes in any size(s) you like. Make sure that your box can be closed to make six sides (just like a Rubik's Cube). Larger boxes make striking decorations, but smaller ones are fun, too!

Poster board in each of the following colors: red, orange, green, blue, white, and yellow

Ruler and pencil

Black electrical tape

Masking tape, two-sided tape, or anything that will work to attach the poster board to the box

Scissors

How to Make

1. Close up your box and tape it shut.

2. Measure one of the sides of your box. (As it is square, all six sides should measure the same.) Using your ruler and pencil, draw a square of that size on each piece of poster board. Cut out the square of each color.

3. Attach one poster board square to each side of the box.

4. Using an actual Rubik's Cube (or a picture of one—there are lots of them online) for reference, use the electrical tape to create black borders around the edges of each of the box sides.

5. Using strips of the electrical tape, divide each box side into 9 colored squares by running two pieces of the tape horizontally across each side, and two pieces vertically (if you want it to look precise, use the ruler to measure, and lightly pencil in where you want your tape to go). It will be like creating a tic-tac-toe board over each of the colored sides. Make sure your pieces reach from one side of the black border to the other.

6. Voilà! You can create just one box, or lots of them to place throughout your party. You can also stack them on top of each other for one gnarly focal piece.

More Awesome '80s Decoration Ideas

• Neon balloons, cups, plates, and other party essentials are always fun for an '80s theme!

• You can buy posters with '80s movie, music, and pop-culture themes online at lots of different websites. Cover your walls with as many as you can get your hands on!

• Create your own posters, using bright or neon colors, with each featuring an '80s slang word, such as *Totally! Gnarly! Awesome! Rad!*

• Display '80s fashion throughout your party. Some items you could look for are slotted shutter-shade neon sunglasses, neon leg warmers, lacy finger-less gloves, brightly colored wigs, ripped jeans, shirts with shoulder pads, and neon anything!

Record Bowls

If you have access to old records, you can make bowls out of them. It's easy, and they make great '80s-themed containers for chips, pretzels, and other munchies. Your friends will be impressed with your creativity, and they'll want to know your secret! Remember to ask your parents for permission to melt records in their oven, and have an adult supervise the activity—no doy!

What You Need

Old vinyl records (Cheap vinyl records can often be found at local thrift stores; look for '80s albums, preferably with cool labels, because they will be seen at the bottoms of your bowls.)
An oven-safe bowl the size you would like your record bowl to be
Cookie sheet
Oven mitts

How to Make

1. Preheat your oven to 200°F.
2. Place the oven-safe bowl upside down on the cookie sheet.
3. Place the record on top of the bowl, making sure that the hole is centered over the center of the bowl's base.

4. Bake for 6–9 minutes. Keep a close eye on it, as some records start to melt faster than others. The record will get soft, and melt enough to droop and form over the bowl. Don't let it melt too much!

5. Wearing oven mitts, remove the cookie sheet with the bowl on it from the oven. Place it on a trivet or another heat-safe surface.

6. Still wearing your oven mitts, carefully peel the record from the outside of the bowl. Flip the bowl back over, and place the record inside the bowl. You now have a short amount of time to mold the record as you like it inside the bowl before it hardens. If it hardens before you are satisfied with its shape, you can place it back in the oven for a few minutes to soften it up again.

7. Once your record has completely cooled and hardened, you can wash and dry it, and put your chosen snacks inside it.

'80s Music!

Putting together an awesomely '80s playlist to set the mood is a must! Make sure you include some hits from the famous music icons that ruled the decade:

- Madonna
- Michael Jackson
- Air Supply
- Prince
- U2

- The Police
- Aerosmith
- R.E.M.
- Bon Jovi
- Whitney Houston

Far-Out Food

Pac-Man was a popular arcade and video game in the '80s, and it's still considered a classic today! If you're not familiar with the game, the player controls a yellow character called Pac-Man through a maze, eating pac-dots (or pellets). How cool would it be to have a cake made to look like Pac-Man, along with frosted cupcakes to represent the pellets? It's totally easy to make!

What You Need

2 boxes of your favorite flavor cake mix, plus all the ingredients and supplies listed on the box—typically, eggs, and oil or butter (one box for the cake, and one for the cupcakes)

2 (16-ounce) tubs of yellow cake frosting (If you can't find yellow frosting, you can color white frosting with yellow food coloring.)

Large round cake pan (One box of cake mix makes two 8" rounds, but pans come in various sizes—it's a good rule of thumb not to fill your pan past the halfway point, to allow for any rising.)

Cupcake pan (One box of cake mix makes about 18–24 regular-sized cupcakes, depending on how much batter you use for each individual cupcake.)

Cupcake liners (yellow if available)

One chocolate sandwich cookie

How to Make

1. Bake the large round cake following the directions on the cake mix box.

2. Let the cake cool completely.

3. Bake the cupcakes according to the directions on the box.

4. Let the cupcakes cook completely.

5. After the large round cake has cooled, cut out a large wedge to create Pac-Man's mouth. Insert a knife into the center of the cake and carefully make one cut to the cake's edge. Insert the knife into the center of the cake again, but angle your cut so that it ends in a different place to create the wedge shape. The exact angle of the wedge doesn't need to be precise; Pac-Man opens and closes his mouth at different angles to eat the pac-dots. But take a look at some pictures online to get a sense of how wide an angle you want to use. Remove the wedge from the cake. (What do you do with it? You eat it, of course!)

6. Use the yellow frosting to cover the entire top of the cake and sides, including the sides of the wedge.

7. Place the chocolate sandwich cookie on the cake as Pac-Man's eye. (In early versions of the Pac-Man game, he had an eye, but in later versions he had none.)

8. After the cupcakes have cooled, frost them, too.

9. When you're ready to display these treats for your friends, line up the cupcakes as if they were the pellets from the game, and Pac-Man is in pursuit to eat them!

'80s Movie-Themed Snacks

These treats are perfect while watching '80s movies! You might want to make labels for them, so that your friends are in on the joke.

- **Breakfast Club Sandwiches:** Create club sandwiches by layering your choice of lunchmeats, cheeses, bacon, lettuce, tomato, and condiments on toast.
- **Three Amigos Salsa and Chips:** Provide three different kinds of salsa and tortilla chips for your guests.
- Easy snacks that don't take much extra work can be renamed to fit the movie, such as **Mystic Pizza Rolls**, **Pretty in Pink Lemonade**, or **Bill and Ted's Excellent Brownies**.

As-If Activities

The '80s party theme offers tons of opportunity for activities to celebrate the gnarliest decade of them all. Here are just a few ideas worth considering.

Best Dressed

Encourage your friends to arrive in style . . . '80s style, that is! The '80s were a decade of unforgettable fashion. Think neon, bright makeup, spandex, leg warmers, ripped jeans, big hair, side ponytails, rubber bracelets, fingerless gloves, slatted sunglasses . . . the list goes on and on. To get your friends to go all out, offer fun prizes in different categories, but don't tell them what the categories are until they arrive. Some ideas to get you started are:

- Loudest makeup
- Best '80s outfit
- Biggest hair
- Most pieces of jewelry

Polaroid Picture Fun

Polaroid instant snapshots were all the rage in the '80s, because they made it easy for people to see their pictures right away instead of having to wait for them to be developed. You can create a life-size Polaroid picture photo prop by using a large white foam board to create a border like the one found on an old Polaroid picture, with even borders on the top and sides, and a wider border across the bottom (you can find examples online). Using an actual or online example as a reference, cut out the square where the "picture" would be, and write the date of your sleepover in the wider, bottom part of the white border, like many people did on actual Polaroid pictures. Let your friends hold the border in front of them to pose for photos that you can take with a digital camera, phone, or tablet to share memories of your good times!

Skills of the '80s Games

- **Lip-Syncing Contest:** Put together a playlist of popular '80s hit songs. Let your friends pick their favorite ones to lip-sync along with. Have everyone perform, then vote for the person whose lips and moves were the best!

- **Learn '80s Dance Moves:** If you know someone that can do awesome '80s dance moves, see if you can get her to come over to your sleepover and show you how to perform some fun moves. If not, you can watch a tutorial on the Internet, and try them out together. Clear a large space on the floor, put on the music, and let any of your friends that are bold enough show off their moves! A few famous dance moves you might want to try are break dancing, the Cabbage Patch, the Electric Slide, the Moon Walk, the Robot, the Sprinkler, and the Worm.

- **Air Guitar Contest:** Break out some loud '80s rock and let your friends jam along with their air guitars. The one who puts on the best show wins!

Pin the Glove on Michael Jackson

This is a much cooler version of the classic game of Pin the Tail on the Donkey. Blindfold each of your friends, then have them try and pin the sequined glove on the Michael Jackson poster without peeking. The girl who comes closest to landing her glove on the right part of the poster wins!

What You Need

Michael Jackson poster (make sure the pose features a prominent hand). You can find these online.

Poster board or card stock

Scissors

Sequins (optional)

Glue (optional)

Tape

Blindfold

Set Up

1. Create gloves by cutting them out of poster board. Make sure they are relatively close to the size and shape of the hand shown on the poster. You can trace over the hand on the poster first to make a template, if you like.

2. Use glue to cover each of the paper gloves with sequins. (You don't have to do this step, but it adds to the fun of the game.)

3. Hang the poster on your wall. Remember, your friends will be blindfolded when they play this game. You will want to hang it somewhere that doesn't have items near it that can be knocked over or damaged.

How to Play

• When you're ready to play, blindfold one of your friends, making sure that she can't see.

• Hand the player a sequined glove (with a piece of rolled-up tape on the back so that it will stick to the poster).

• Spin each player around three times to disorient her. Now, point her in the direction of the poster, and let her stick the glove where she thinks the hand is.

• Let each friend have a turn. The glove closest to the hand wins, of course!

Classic '80s Board Games

Another idea is to play the games that were popular at parties in the '80s. Here are some games that are still being sold today:

- Twister
- Pictionary
- Mouse Trap
- Operation

- Life
- Topple
- Trivial Pursuit

'80s Movies

Once you've put on your PJs and are ready to settle down for the night, it's the perfect time to watch a movie, so put on an '80s classic. Here are a few great suggestions; line up some of your movie-themed snacks, and you're all set!

- *Sixteen Candles*
- *Bill & Ted's Excellent Adventure*
- *The Breakfast Club*
- *Ghostbusters*

- *The Goonies*
- *Mystic Pizza*
- *Pretty in Pink*
- *The Three Amigos*

Favors

After your totally awesome party, you'll want to give your guests a little parting favor to remember their trip back in time. One great idea is to fill a favor bag with some fun '80s mementoes like:

- Slotted shutter-shade glasses
- Hair scrunchies
- Rubber bracelets
- Neon nail polish

- Rubik's Cube keychain
- Slinky
- Handheld Pac-Man game

Chapter 9

Hollywood Glitz and Glam Sleepover

If you have found yourself dreaming of what life in Hollywood would be like, then use that dream to live out an unforgettable night with your friends. A Hollywood glitz and glam sleepover will have you and your friends rolling out the red carpet and stepping into the glamorous life for a night, focused on feeling like a star.

VIP Pass Invitations

Get out the velvet rope—only very important people are invited to this epic party! Let your friends know they are in for a posh night by sending out a VIP invitation that will set the tone for your star-studded sleepover. You can even require that they bring it along in order to gain access to your Hollywood event.

What You Need
Black card stock
Star stickers
Self-sealing laminating pouches (business card size)
Gold paint marker
Scissors
Hole punch
Lanyards, ribbons, or yarn (one for each invitation)

How to Make

1. Cut black card stock into 2" x 3" pieces, one for each invitation. (Measure your self-sealing laminating pouches to make sure this size will fit. Adjust your measurements if necessary.)

2. On one side of each piece of cut card stock, use the gold paint marker to write down the details of the party. Make sure to say that they will need to bring the pass for admission!

3. On the other side of each piece of card stock, write "VIP pass" and any extra details you may want to include.

4. Place the star stickers on both sides of the invitation for an added touch of glitz.

5. Slide each invitation into the self-sealing laminating pouches. Follow the directions on the package to seal them.

6. Use the hole punch to make a hole at the top of each invite and attach them to the lanyard, ribbon, or yarn. That way your friends can wear them during the party.

L.A. Menu

As you plan your menu for the party, think of the foods that you can serve to suit the Hollywood theme. Hollywood is associated with movies, lights, and fame, so dressing up some simple finger foods should have your friends in awe and leave your budget intact.

Star-Studded Delights

These yummy treats are sure to hit the spot . . . spotlight that is!

What You Need

Lunchmeat of your choice
Chive and onion cream cheese
Star-shaped cookie cutter

Spread cream cheese over a piece of lunchmeat. Layer three pieces of the cheese and meat, and top with one plain piece of meat. Cut a star out using the cookie cutter and place on a foil-covered plate to give that Hollywood glitz everyone loves.

Golden Nuggets

What's better than popcorn? Popcorn with a deliciously sweet coating! Ask an adult for help making this snack; hot honey and butter can splatter or burn.

What You Need

Roasting pan lined with wax paper
20 cups popped popcorn
¾ cup butter, divided (see next page)

1¼ cups honey
¾ teaspoon salt
2 teaspoons vanilla extract

1. Begin by heating your oven to 325°F. Place the already popped popcorn in the lined roasting pan.

2. In a saucepan over medium heat, combine ½ cup of the butter, all of the honey and salt, then stir until butter is melted, then stir in vanilla extract.

3. Pour the mixture over the popcorn and then bake for 25 minutes, stirring occasionally. Remove from the oven and let cool for 5 minutes.

4. Make sure the popcorn has cooled enough to handle safely. Coat your hands in the remaining butter and roll the popcorn into 2-inch balls. Place the popcorn balls onto the wax paper to set.

5. Once they are cool and have set, place the golden nuggets into small bags for your friends to grab and snack on.

Red Carpet Salsa

This salsa is best if displayed in a rectangular dish, to look like the red carpet! Ask an adult for supervision and help using the blender.

What You Need
6 Roma tomatoes
⅓ cup chopped onion
1 bunch of cilantro
3 garlic cloves
1 lime
Pinch each of salt and cayenne pepper
1 chopped jalapeno (optional)

1. In a blender, combine the tomatoes, chopped onion, cilantro, and garlic, and pulsate three or four times.

2. Squeeze the juice of the lime over the mix with a couple of pinches of salt and a pinch of cayenne pepper, and blend for 10 seconds. If you want some kick to your salsa, add in 1 chopped jalapeno when blending.

3. Serve chilled with tortilla chips or mini bagels for delicious dipping.

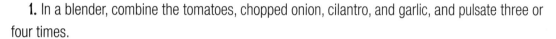

Pink "Champagne"

A delicious fruity punch to quench the thirst of celebrities and their fans alike!

What You Need

1 (12-ounce) can of frozen pink lemonade
1 quart club soda, chilled
4 cups white cranberry juice cocktail

1. In either a punch bowl or large pitcher, combine the thawed pink lemonade, chilled club soda, and white cranberry juice.

2. Mix well. Serve chilled in plastic champagne glasses, or have punch cups available. You can usually find the plastic glassware at a party store or local dollar stores.

Tuxedo Cookies

Hollywood is a black- and white-tie affair, so that calls for some fancy cookies for you and your friends. Ask an adult for help melting the chocolate.

What You Need

Bag of semi-sweet, milk, or dark chocolate chips
Bag of white chocolate chips
Sugar cookies
Waxed paper

1. In 2 separate bowls, melt the bag of chocolate chips and the bag of white chocolate chips. Microwave on high for 45 seconds, stir, and continue microwaving for 15-second intervals until the chocolate is completely melted.

2. Spread the sugar cookies out on wax paper, leaving about an inch or two between each cookie.

3. Dip half of each cookie in chocolate, let the chocolate set, and then dip the other half in white chocolate. When the chocolate has set, your tuxedo cookies are ready to be devoured.

Decorations

It's amazing how easy it can be to decorate for a Hollywood glitz and glam sleepover. Gold, black, and silver are often colors associated with this theme, but you can use whatever colors you think are glamorous. Try these ideas:

• Use a clapperboard (found at your local party store or online) as a centerpiece. Some clapperboards are made with a chalkboard paint finish, so you can write your name or a message on it for a more authentic look.

• Create a red carpet using a roll of red paper and some double-sided tape to keep it adhered to the floor. You can also check your local party stores to see if they have disposable red carpets available for purchase.

• Cut out stars of varying sizes using different colors of foil paper or card stock. Use a hole punch to make a hole in one tip of each star, and run a piece of fishing line through each one to create star garland. You can also hang single stars to create the feel of floating stars.

• Spread star-shaped confetti or shiny shred on your food table to give a little pizzazz and sparkle to the table itself.

• Print out pictures of several famous individuals and post them all over the party room.

• Use shiny doorway fringe of your color choice to create a grand entrance to your party.

Games

Let the games begin! Time to play some Hollywood style games.

Acceptance Speech

This is a game that will test how quickly your friends can think on their feet, and make for some fun and unforgettable laughs.

What You Need

An index card for each friend   *A pen for each friend*   *A bowl or hat*

How to Play

1. Have each person write down the name of a movie she likes, but tweaking the title to make it funny. Follow that title with a one-sentence description of the fake film. For example, they could write down "*Mean Curls*, a film about a group of cruel but popular wigs who rule their high school with an iron hairbrush."

2. Once everyone has written down their ideas, fold up the cards and place them in the bowl or hat.

3. The first person pulls a card and reads it aloud to the group, then makes up an award acceptance speech as if they were the main character in the movie.

4. At the end, have everyone vote on who had the best speech! You can offer a small prize for the winner.

Hollywood Couple Shuffle

Keeping up with what's hot and what's not is just part of loving Hollywood life. This game will see just how up to date your friends are on Hollywood's best couples.

What You Need

Pictures of several celebrity couples. You will also need a picture of each person from each couple, by themselves. (For example, if you have a picture of Angelina Jolie and Brad Pitt, you'll need a separate photo of Angelina and a separate photo of Brad, as well.)
Pen
Paper
Timer

How to Play

1. Before your party, prepare the photos. Take each picture of the solo celebrities and write a different letter on the back of each one. On the back of the pictures of the couples, write the letters of the celebrities that go together. For example, you'd write A on the back of Angelina Jolie's photo, and B on the back of Brad Pitt's photo. On the back of the photo of Angelina and Brad together, you'd write A + B.

2. Shuffle the single photos really well and stack them face up. Place the stack of the celebrity couples face down.

3. When it's time to play, place the stack of solo celebrity photos face down in the center of the table. Take the pictures of the celebrity couples standing together and put them in a stack face down to one side. No peeking!

4. Set the timer for 2 minutes, and have someone volunteer to be the first to go. Each person will have 2 minutes to go through the stack of solo celebrities and write down the letters of the celebrities that she believes are a couple. She can spread the pictures out or use whatever method she likes to come to her conclusions, but beware! Others are watching!

5. Once everyone has had their turn, take the stack of couple photos. Hold up the first photo of a celebrity couple and call out the letters so everyone can check them against their lists. The person with the most correct answers wins!

Who's Got Talent?

This is a fun game that will bring out talents in your friends that you may not have known about.

How to Play

1. Before starting this game, you will need to ask two to three people to volunteer to be the judges for the game. If there are adults or older siblings available, you can ask them to be judges so that all of your friends can participate.

2. Give everyone participating 5 minutes to come up with a personal routine for a talent show. Each routine must last no longer than 3 minutes, and can be whatever is suitable for your surroundings. You might want to have a selection of music available in case someone wants to sing, do a dance interpretation, or rock out on the air guitar.

3. Let everyone present their talent in front of the group. Remember that it takes a lot of courage to perform in front of people, don't make it any harder by heckling the performer. Even if you are just joking it could hurt feelings. Have everyone encourage and cheer on everyone else. After all that is what friends are for.

4. At the end you can have the judges give out awards for best act, funniest, most athletic, etc.

Who's Who?

Starting a game right when your friends arrive is a good way to set the tone for the evening, and this is the game to get it started right.

What You Need

Paper

Pen

Clothespins or safety pins

How to Play

1. Before your sleepover begins, write a different name of a celebrity on each piece of paper. It's good to list a variety of celebrities including musicians, actors/actresses, comedians, and socialites that are currently in the limelight.

2. As your friends arrive, pin a paper with a celebrity name to their back without letting them see the name. Make sure to explain the rules to the game: they have to guess which celebrity they are by asking "yes" or "no" questions using the first person pronoun. For example, someone could say, "Am I a singer in a band?" No one is allowed to tell another person who they are; they can only answer the "yes" or "no" questions.

3. Once a person is confident that they know which celebrity she is, she can ask the final question of, "Am I . . . ?" If they get it wrong, then they're out! The ones who guess correctly win a small prize.

Activities

Back to the Future

This activity will have everyone curious as to what the future holds for them, because it is truly out of their hands.

What You Need

Blank paper   *Pens*   *Timer*

How to Play

1. Have everyone sit in a circle.

2. Give each person a pen and a sheet of paper. A hard surface to write on helps.

3. Set the timer for 10 minutes. Everyone has that long to write a biography of the person to her right. The biography is based on the life she has yet to live. This can be a prediction of her real future, or made into something a bit comical. The one rule is that you can't write anything hurtful or mean.

4. Once the time is up, everyone will pass her notebook to the left.

5. One by one, each guest will read the biography handed to her out loud to the group and find out what was predicted for her future life.

Lights, Camera, Action

Have your friends gather for a walk down the red carpet with this activity!

What You Need

Red carpet. This can be simply a designated walking path, or you can go all out and have an actual red carpet. One economical way to create this is by joining red plastic tablecloths together (the kind sold at your local dollar store are perfect).

Several cameras (You can ask your friends to bring their own to help out, or use phones or tablets for digital pictures you can share with one another; you can also use disposable cameras that will need to be taken in for traditional print photos to be developed.)

Assortment of wearable props, like sunglasses, hats, boas, costume jewelry

Toy microphones (or something to act as a microphone, like a brush)

How to Play

1. Have your friends decide if they want to walk down the red carpet as a pair or as singles. Everyone else will be paparazzi. Some will have cameras to take pictures, and some will have microphones to interview the celebrity/celebrities.

2. Each celebrity will have a couple of minutes to go through the props before she takes her walk down the carpet, so that she can look her best.

3. Once everyone has taken their walk, you can use the pictures to review and have a good laugh.

Walk of Fame

This activity will give everyone her very own star on Hollywood Boulevard!

What You Need

Construction paper　　　　*Paint*　　　　*Permanent marker*
Scissors　　　　*Plate*

How to Play

1. Use the scissors to cut out a large star shape from the construction paper. You will need one for each of your friends.

2. Pour some paint on a plate, and spread it around by moving the plate in a circular motion.

3. Using the marker, each person writes her name on her star.

4. Taking turns, each person then dips her hand in the paint, and places it on her star to make a handprint.

5. Set the stars aside to dry. Later, everyone can marvel at their very own stars on their walk of fame and stage fun photos with them.

Favors

Getting together a favor bag for your Hollywood glitz and glam sleepover is super easy! With the activities suggested for this theme, your guests probably already have something to take home, but in case you would like to include more, here are a few suggestions:

- Glitter lip gloss
- Toy microphones
- Cool glasses
- Plastic top hats
- Party beads
- Little compact mirrors
- Mini clapperboards
- Fake mustaches
- Shiny hair bows
- Rings or bracelets
- Star-shaped erasers
- Nail polish

Chapter 10

Fear Factor Fun Sleepover

Is fear a factor for you and your friends? Invite them to a sleepover party they will never forget! This is no place for the weak-hearted; only the courageous need apply. The idea of a fear factor party is to have different games, activities, and even foods to test your friends' daring and courage.

Creepy Crawly Invitations

Set the tone for your bash with an invitation that comes with a frightful surprise!

What You Need

Cardboard tubes from toilet paper rolls, enough for each invitation you plan to make

Plastic bugs or spiders

Yellow tissue paper

Black ribbon

Notecard (or notecard-size printout) with party details written on it

How to Make

1. Fold up the card with the party details and slide it inside the empty cardboard tube.

2. Use tissue paper to wrap around the cardboard tube. Leave about 2½" of tissue paper extending past each end. Twist one end of the tissue paper, wrap a ribbon around the twist, and tie to secure.

3. Insert a few of the plastic bugs or spiders into the cardboard tube through the open end.

4. Twist the open end closed and secure with ribbon, just like you did on the other side.

5. Tell your friends to open the tubes by pulling on each end of the twisted tissue paper. The bugs will pop out, giving them a hint of what is in store for them if they have the guts to come to your fear factor sleepover!

Ghoulish Menu

The following menu items all have one thing in common. They all sound gross and look gross, but taste delicious!

Brains

Using a brain mold, you can make this a treat you and your friends will not forget.

What You Will Need

Specialty gelatin brain mold (You can find these online.)

Oil cooking spray

3 large (6-ounce) or 6 small (3-ounce) watermelon-flavored gelatin packs

2½ cups boiling water

1 cup cold water

1 (12-ounce) can light or fat-free evaporated milk

Green food coloring

Kitchen towel

Mixing bowl

Mixing bowl large enough for the brain mold to fit inside

Serving platter

Garnishes (see final step)

How to Make

1. Start with a clean brain mold. Spray the inside with cooking spray.

2. In a large bowl, mix the gelatin powder and boiling water until the powder is completely dissolved.

3. Stir in 1 cup of cold water and the evaporated milk to the mix. Stir well.

4. Add 5–6 drops of green food coloring to create the fleshy tone of brain.

5. Place a kitchen towel in the bottom of a mixing bowl. This bowl should be just big enough to fit the brain mold inside. Set aside.

6. Pour mixture into the brain mold. Make sure to leave 1" of space at the top, so that it will not spill when you move it.

7. Carefully place the brain mold into the bowl. Use the kitchen towel to keep the mold upright as it sets. Place in the refrigerator and let set for at least 4 hours.

8. When the gelatin has set, you will need to carefully extract it from the plastic mold. Shake the mold a bit to loosen the gelatin, and then turn over onto your serving dish.

9. Garnish as you would like. Some ideas include placing kale leaves around it, or gummy worms, or covering it with red food coloring to give it a bloody look.

Diaper Surprise

These chocolate surprises have the biggest gross-out effect if you use actual clean diapers to display them on instead of serving dishes. Remember to ask your parents for help melting the chocolate in the microwave.

What You Need
12 pre-made rice cereal treats
2-pound bag milk chocolate wafers
2 clean diapers

How to Make
1. With clean hands, take each individual rice cereal treat and squeeze it into an irregular shape. Long and lumpy is what you are going for.

2. Melt the milk chocolate wafers in microwave according to directions.

3. Dip each rice cereal treat into chocolate. Place on parchment paper to dry. It should only take a few minutes before the chocolate has hardened and created a delicious shell on the rice cereal treats.

4. That's it! Store them in refrigerator until you are ready to serve them, to your friends' disgust and delight. When the time comes, open up the diapers and pile the treats on top. Mmmmmm . . . .

Dirty Q-Tips

They look so gross, but taste SO good. This gross-out recipe creates what first appears to be large Q-tips with great globs of earwax on them, but if you are brave enough to try them you will find yummy marshmallows dipped in caramel. Remember to ask for help from your parents to melt the caramels in the microwave.

What You Need

Small container of caramel dip (individually wrapped candies, or caramel baking bits)
50 miniature marshmallows (this makes 25 dirty Q-tips)
Toothpicks (1 for every 2 marshmallows)
Baking sheet or platter lined with waxed paper

How to Make

1. Attach a miniature marshmallow to each end of a toothpick. Make several. Dip the ends of the marshmallow into caramel dip. You don't need to coat the whole marshmallow in caramel; just a clump on the ends will do.

2. Lay on the waxed paper–covered platter while you make more. Place the platter of treats to store until party time.

3. When it's time to serve them, display spread out haphazardly on a serving dish.

Kitty Litter Cake

What would your friends think if they walked into your party and saw, sitting on your table along with all your other fiendish fear factor treats, a litter box filled with what appeared to be used kitty litter? This cake is sure to bring mixed reactions from your friends, but if any of them are daring enough to try it, they will discover pure deliciousness. Remember to ask your parents for help using the microwave, food processor, and oven!

What You Need

New, unused litter box and scoop (wash both in hot soapy water before using them)
2 boxes marble cake mix
1 (12-ounce) package peanut butter sandwich cookies (You can use vanilla if any friends have food allergies.)
Green food coloring
3 Butterfinger candy bars
4 snack-pack size containers of vanilla pudding
8 small Tootsie Rolls

How to Make

1. Bake cake according to box directions. It doesn't matter what shape you bake it in, because you'll be crumbling it up later.

2. Crush the cookies. If you have a food processor, use it to crumble them. If you don't have a food processor you can put all the cookies in a zip-top bag, close it securely, and crush the cookies with your hands or a rolling pin.

3. Take ¼ cup of the crushed cookies and place in a small bowl. Add 3–4 drops of green food coloring to it and mix well. Set aside.

4. Crumble the Butterfinger bars. You can use a food processor for this task as well, but again if you don't have a food processor you can use the bag method as described in Step 2. Place in a bowl and set aside.

5. When cakes have cooled to room temperature, crumble them into litter box. Mix in the pudding cups, crumbled candy bars, and ½ of the untinted crushed cookie mixture.

6. Unwrap the Tootsie Rolls and place them on a small microwave-safe plate. Heat the Tootsie Rolls a few seconds at a time in the microwave until they are soft enough to mold (it won't take long). Mold them so that they curve slightly and all the ends are rounded. You could also twist some into swirls. Get creative. (You know what shape you're looking for here!)

7. Spread the Tootsie Roll shapes on top of the cake, along with the rest of the crushed cookies and the green cookie mix.

8. Serve the cake dessert with a litter scoop for a treat that your friends will never forget!

Bloody Fingers

Mozzarella cheese sticks and lunchmeat come together to look like flesh falling off the bone. This will yield 12 fingers.

What You Need

12 mozzarella cheese sticks
Knife
Barbecue sauce
12 thinly sliced light-colored lunchmeat (such as turkey or chicken)
12 almond slices

How to Make

1. Unwrap all the cheese sticks.

2. Spread the barbecue sauce thinly on one side of a slice of lunchmeat. Wrap the meat around a cheese stick. The barbecue sauce will help it stick.

3. Once the meat is wrapped around the cheese, use the knife to slash the meat in a couple of places to give it a ragged appearance.

4. Stick an almond slice into the tip of the cheese stick to look like a fingernail.

Decorations

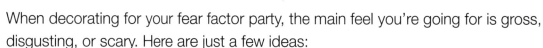

When decorating for your fear factor party, the main feel you're going for is gross, disgusting, or scary. Here are just a few ideas:

• Rubber bugs everywhere! Think spiders, roaches, maggots, and flies. You can put them crawling up walls, chilling on doorknobs, converging on tables . . . let your imagination run wild.

• Instead of hanging balloons from the ceiling, hang plastic skulls and bones instead.

• Fill decorative jars full of novelty toy eyeballs and place around the party tables for ambience.

• Create a banner out of black and yellow posterboard that reads, "What's Your Fear Factor?" or " Face Your Fear Factor!" You'll need at least five sheets each of yellow and black posterboard. Cut each sheet of yellow posterboard into four equal pieces. Cut the letters of your chosen words out of the black posterboard and glue one to each yellow piece. One you have all the letters glued on, punch holes along the top of each piece. String them together and hang the banner where your friends will see it when they first arrive.

• Turn ordinary things into gross things. Do you have a fish tank? Have something gross floating in it. Do you have houseplants? Have something unnatural "growing" out of a few. Do you have mirrors? Have "bloody" handprints smeared across them.

Games

Who has what it takes to face her fears in the following scary, challenging, and downright gross fear factor games?

Iron Toes

In this challenge, your friends test their endurance by sticking their bare feet into ice cold water to retrieve as many marbles as they can from the bottom. Brr!

What You Need
A bucket or tub
Ice
Stopwatch or timer
30–40 marbles
Water

How to Set Up and Play
1. Set up this challenge in a place where you (and your parents) won't mind if some water splashes out, like outside, or perhaps in your bathroom.

2. Place the marbles in the bottom of the bucket. Fill the bucket with half water and half ice.

3. Challenge your friends, one at a time, to reach a bare foot into the icy cold water. They have 1 minute to pull out as many marbles as they can with their toes. You may want to place a small bowl next to the tub so they have something to put the marbles in when they pull them out.

4. After each person has taken her turn, count her marbles and then return them to the tub for the next person. The person who pulls out the most marbles wins!

Worm Pie

By the end of this game, all of your friend's faces will be covered with whipped cream. Make sure you have your camera ready!

What You Need

One pie tin for each player (You can get foil pie plates from the dollar store; you can also use paper plates if you are on a tighter budget, but they won't be as deep.)
Enough whipped cream to fill each pie tin
Gummy worms (3 worms for each pie tin)

How to Set Up and Play

1. Prepare a "pie" for each player by placing three gummy worms at the bottom of each pie tin and covering them with whipped cream.

2. Place the "worm pies" around the table, and have each of your friends take a place in front of one.

3. Everyone must place their hands behind their backs for the duration of the game. No hands can be used! If any of your friends have long hair, have them tie it back before the game begins.

4. Go! The first person to find and eat all three of her gummy worms wins!

Ticket or Cricket

Did you know crickets are more afraid of you than you are of them? Still, this fact might not be comforting when you are trying to stick your hand in a tank full of jumping, frantic crickets. Can your friends face their fear and win the challenge?

What You Need

Empty fish tank with lid
Carnival-type tickets (You can make these yourself or purchase them at a party store.)
At least 100 feeder crickets, the more the better (You can purchase these very cheaply at your local pet store.)
Shredded paper
Stopwatch or timer

How to Set Up and Play

1. Fill your tank with the shredded paper, tickets, and crickets. Keep the lid on until you are ready to begin your challenge. You should purchase your crickets on the day of the party to make sure they stay alive.

2. Challenge each of your friends to reach in with one hand and pull out as many tickets as they can in 1 minute.

3. When your friends reach in the tank, the crickets will actually jump away from their hands, but it's the fear factor that matters. The player who pulls out the most tickets wins! Afterward you can return the crickets to the pet store.

Cat Food Surprise

Do your friends have the guts to eat a spoonful of cat food? You're about to find out!

What You Need

3 small cans of Spam luncheon meat
3 different flavored cans of wet cat food, the same size as the Spam cans (You want to be able to give your friends a choice of which flavor they want to try.)
Transparent tape
Spoons

How to Set Up and Play

1. Before the party, carefully remove the labels from the cat food and use them to replace the labels on the cans of Spam. Use tape to secure. The Spam can is a rectangle and most cat food cans are circular, so you may need to do a bit of finessing to make the illusion believable!

2. Dispose of the evidence that the Spam is anything other than the cat food it is disguised as!

3. Challenge each of your friends to eat a spoonful of cat food.

4. Make sure to open the cans of "cat food" in front of your friends. Make a big show of scooping the spoon into the Spam—I mean, cat food, of course—and handing it to the first daring volunteer.

5. Award a prize or advancement in the games to everyone who is willing and able to actually swallow a bit of "cat food."

Egg Roulette

Are your friends daring enough to crack what could be a raw egg on their head?

What You Need

Boiled eggs (one for each of your friends)

How to Set Up and Play

1. Tell your friends that you have a bowl full of boiled eggs . . . all except one.

2. Have them all sit in a circle. Let each one point to one of the eggs. Place that egg in front of them, but don't allow them to touch it yet.

3. Tell them that they are not allowed to touch the egg until you say go. They then must immediately pick up the egg and crack it on the top of their head. The one that gets the raw egg is out.

4. Of course, all the eggs are boiled, so the true loser of this game is the last one who cracks the egg on their head because they let the fear rule them most!

Baby Food Challenge

In this challenge, your friends will get a chance to test their palates.

What You Need

6 different jars of baby food   *Spoons*

Blindfold   *Pen and paper*

How to Set Up and Play

1. Remove all the labels from the baby food jars and mark the jars with a number instead. Write down which numbered jar contains which food, so you don't forget.

2. Blindfold one of your friends, and feed her a small amount of baby food from each jar. Let her guess what it is, and record her guess next to the jar's number on her paper.

3. When the first person has finished her taste test, blindfold the next person and record her answers. Mix up the order of the jars so that no one can rely on a previous person's guesses! When everyone has had a turn, reveal the contents of each jar. The player with the most correct guesses wins!

Slimy Activity

Icky, sticky, blobby fun—here is a slime-a-licious activity to do with your friends.

Super Slime

This slime is not only fun to make, it's also fun to play with!

What You Need

½ cup nonwashable glue for each friend (don't forget yourself)
1½ cups water, divided
Food coloring (multiple colors your friends can choose from is best)
1 teaspoon Borax detergent for each friend
2 bowls and a spoon for each friend (disposable makes for easy cleanup)
Zip-top bag for each friend to store her slime

How to Make

1. Mix ½ cup glue and ½ cup water together in a bowl.
2. Add food coloring until you reach the color you would like your slime to be.
3. In the other bowl dissolve 1 teaspoon of Borax into 1 cup of water.
4. Pour the glue mixture into the Borax bowl and start stirring and kneading the mixture. Slime will form almost immediately.
5. Pour out any excess water and transfer slime into zip-top bags. You and your friends can now play with the slime. When not using slime store it in zip-top bag to keep it from drying out.

Frightful Favors

If you want to give your friends a parting gift to help them remember their exciting evening, consider a few of the following ideas.

• Have T-shirts printed up for each of your guests reading, "Fear Is Not a Factor for Me!" Underneath it can read, "I survived (your name here)'s Fear Factor Sleepover."

• Take tons of pictures throughout the party and put together a Fear Scrapbook to give each of your friends at a later date.

• A picture frame with plastic creepy crawlies glued onto it makes a great place for a picture taken of you and all your friends at the sleepover.

• A jar filled with realistic-looking gummy worms, with a tag hanging from it reading, "Thanks for facing your fear at (your name here)'s sleepover" makes a sweet treat. You can purchase realistic gummy worms at specialty sites online.

Sugar Rush! A Candy-Themed Sleepover

Sugar, candy, and all things SWEET! That is what this sleepover is all about. What could be better than a party centered around your sweet tooth? A candy-themed party is a great way for you and your friends to celebrate all things sweet, sugary, and delicious! Invite your friends to celebrate the pure rush of sugar with this scrumdiddlyumptious sleepover. From the food to the fun, everything about this party is sugar-tastic!

Candy Invitations

How are you planning to convey your theme in your invitations? Why not do it with actual candy! Design a new label for an ordinary candy bar to create a fun and delicious party invitation.

What You Need

Chocolate bars (one for each friend you would like to invite, plus an extra for measuring)
Card stock or heavy paper
Markers/pens
Ruler
Large label
Transparent tape

How to Make

1. Remove wrapper from one of the candy bars. Use your ruler to measure the full length and width of the wrapper and note it down so you can create your custom wrapper to the same measurements.

2. On a piece of card stock, draw the shape of your wrapper cover using the measurements you just found. Cut out the new wrapper.

3. It's time to get creative! Using your markers and pens, design your candy wrapper. Take your label and write "You are Invited to (your name)'s Birthday Sleepover!" and all your important party details. Decorate the rest of the front with fun creative designs and colors.

4. Glue or tape your label to the center of the card stock wrapper you cut out.

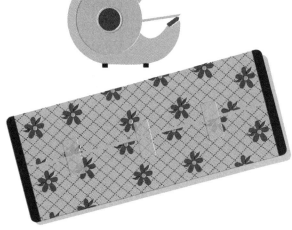

5. You do not need to remove the original wrappers from the candy bars. Simply wrap your new wrapper around the bar, creasing it so that it fits snugly, and secure on the back with transparent tape. Voilà!

Sugar-tastic Menu

You're having a candy party, so of course you want to have tons of sweet treats to offer your friends! Try to have all your friends' favorite candies ready. Consider some of these sweet treat ideas to make things extra special.

- **S'mores Center:** When it gets dark, have your parents set up a small bonfire or charcoal barbecue outside so you and your friends can roast marshmallows for s'mores.
- **Sundae Bar:** Set up a sundae bar where your friends can make their own sundaes. Make sure to have plenty of candy toppings available.
- **Cupcake Station:** Let your friends decorate their own previously frosted cupcakes with a variety of candy toppings, or provide tubes of colored frosting and let them pile it on their own before adding decorations. Turn it into a fun contest and vote to see whose is the best.

Decorations

Candy, candy everywhere! Turn your party into a candy wonderland with these fun and delicious-looking DIY ideas.

Giant Cotton Candy Clouds

Create giant clouds that look like cotton candy using the stuffing for plush toys or pillows and spray paint. Remember to ask an adult for help and supervision for this project.

What You Need

Polyfill stuffing (You can find this in the craft section of a sewing or hobby shop.)

Spray paint in the colors you want your cotton candy to be (Pale pink and blue are the most common.)

Mask and gloves
Clear pushpins

How to Make

1. Pull apart handfuls of your stuffing and shape it into a puff or cloud.

2. Take your clouds outside and spread out some newspaper or a drop cloth. Put on a mask and gloves to use the spray paint. Spray-paint the stuffing in the color desired. If you have created more than one "cloud" you can spray-paint each a different color. Don't oversaturate the clouds; use a light hand to tint them. Allow to dry.

3. Once it's dry, bring your cotton candy cloud inside and pin it to the ceiling using clear pushpins.

Gumball Garland

String a gumball garland across your party area or around your buffet table for a fun and yummy detail.

What You Need

A large amount of multicolored gumballs (the more gumballs you have, the longer your garland can be)

Fishing line or dental floss

Large clean sewing needle

Two small sticks (lollipop sticks or toothpicks work well)

How to Make

1. Decide how long you want your garland to be, and cut a piece of string (fishing line or dental floss work great) to that length.

2. Thread your string through the eye of the needle. On the other end of the string, tie a knot around a small item, such as a lollipop stick, so that the gumballs cannot fall off once strung.

3. Decide if you want to create your garland in a pattern or in random order. Once you know how you want your garland to look, you can begin stringing your gumballs.

4. To string the gumballs, simply insert your needle into the gumball and push it out through the opposite side. Slide the gumball down the string, and add the next gumball.

5. Continue until you have either strung all the gumballs or you've reached the length you want. Remove the needle and tie the loose end of the string around another small item, such as another lollipop stick, to ensure that the gumballs do not slide off the string.

Lollipop Lanterns

Turn ordinary party lanterns into cool lollipop lights with this easy trick.

What You Need

Party lantern(s)

Clear cellophane wrap

Ribbon

¾-inch white dowel stick(s), length approximately 24 inches (If you can't find them in white, you can paint them white yourself.)

How to Make

1. Cover your lantern in cellophane wrap. Use enough so that you can secure at the bottom and there is a bit sticking out just like an actual lollipop wrapper.

2. Insert dowel stick through the bottom where you have tied off the cellophane. Use tape to secure firmly together.

3. Tie a ribbon around the cellophane where the lantern meets the dowel stick.

4. Hang the lollipop lantern just as you would a regular paper lantern.

Candy Topiary Centerpieces

These fantastic centerpieces made from colorful candy pieces and topiary balls are a feast for the eyes!

What You Need

Topiary balls of different sizes

Colorful candy such as Skittles, Nerds, and Dum Dum–style lollipops

¾-inch dowel sticks, approximately 12 inches in length

Hot glue gun and glue sticks

Glass beads (enough to fill your chosen vases or flowerpots)

Vases or flowerpots

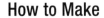

How to Make

1. Insert dowel stick into the topiary ball. Do not push the dowel stick all the way through. It should resemble a large lollipop.

2. Choose one kind of candy for each ball. Glue the pieces of the candy onto the ball leaving no space in between each piece. If you're worried that the topiary ball will show through with the type of candy you are using, you might want to paint the ball beforehand with a complementary color of acrylic paint. If you are using lollipops, you do not need to attach them with hot glue; you can simply insert the stick all the way into the foam ball to secure them.

3. Once you have made a variety of different candy-covered topiary balls, you can insert them into different vases or flowerpots to display them. To do this you will need to stabilize the dowel stick inside the vase to keep the ball upright. This can be done by filling the vase or container with glass beads before inserting the other end of the dowel stick into the vase.

Giant Candy Cane

Giant candy canes are easy to make with pool noodles and ribbon!

What You Need

Red pool noodles (with hollow core)   *Straight pins*
White ribbon   *Fishing line*

How to Make

1. Bend the top of your pool noodle into a curve to form the shape of a candy cane. Tie fishing line to the end of the candy cane's hook, and tie the other end across from it on the main staff to secure the curve. (If you don't do this, your pool noodle will pop back into its original straight shape.)

2. Insert the end of the white ribbon into the hollow core and secure it there with a straight pin. Wind the ribbon around and down the noodle like a candy-cane stripe, using additional straight pins to secure it along the way. When you reach the other end of the noodle, cut off the excess ribbon and insert the cut end into the hollow core. Secure it with a straight pin, and you are finished!

3. These are great for creating an entrance way to your door, or simply hanging in the party area for added ambience!

Hard Candy Balloons

Dress up your balloons to match your sugarlicious theme!

What You Need

Balloons   *Clear cellophane wrap*   *Ribbons*

How to Make

Simply wrap each balloon in cellophane, with the ends of the cellophane open on both sides. Make sure there's extra cellophane extending past the balloon on those sides; these will become the twists like a hard candy wrapper. Gather each open end together close to the balloon, and tie a ribbon around the gathered part to secure the twist. Fluff out the open edge of the gathered cellophane. They should look like giant pieces of hard candy!

Candy Collage Banner

Create a candy banner of your name to celebrate your big day!

What You Need

Posterboard sheets (one for each letter in your name)	*Scissors*	*Glue*
	A variety of hard candy (You	*Hole punch*
Pencil	*can also use images of candy.)*	*Ribbon or string*

How to Make

1. Draw each letter of your name on the posterboard, and cut each letter out. (You can use all one color, but it looks super cool if you use different colors for each letter.)

2. Now get started covering each letter with real candy and images of candy. If you like, you can find and cut out words associated with your theme, like "yummy," "delicious," "sweet," and so on. You can put whatever you wish on your collage, so have fun with it!

3. Once you have finished and all the glue has dried, punch holes in the top of your letters. Take a length of ribbon and thread it through the holes so that the letters hang from it.

4. Hang your banner and get the party started!

More Decorating Ideas

A few more decorating ideas to turn your party room into a giant candy land:

- **Giant Lollipops:** To make giant lollipops, simply tape a balloon onto one end of a wrapping paper tube that you've painted white, then wrap the balloon with clear cellophane. Gather the cellophane where the balloon meets the tube, and tie a ribbon or string to secure it.
- **Jellybean Raindrops:** Unbend one half of a white paperclip. Stick the straightened end through a jellybean, and tie clear fishing line through the looped end of the paperclip. Fasten the loose end of the string to the ceiling to make the jellybean appear as if it's falling from the cotton candy clouds. Make a couple of dozen jellybean raindrops, and hang them at different heights.
- **Candy Replicas:** Re-create your favorite candy packages using posterboard, markers, and some creative elbow grease.

Games

Now that you and your friends are on a sugar rush from eating all that candy it is time to expel some of that energy with some candy-centric games!

Candy Scavenger Hunt Relay Race

In this game, players are given short riddles. Each riddle's answer is the name of a type of candy. Teams must rush to find the correct candy and bring it back to the starting point in order to get the next clue. The first team to get all ten riddles correct wins!

What You Need

2 of each type of candy—Almond Joy bar, Bit-O-Honey, Snickers bar, Crunch bar, Lemonheads, Milky Way bar, Mounds bar, 3 Musketeers bar, Whoppers, Zero bar

2 large tubs or buckets

Easter grass or shredded paper

How to Play

1. Put one of each candy type into each bucket. Fill the remainder of the buckets with Easter grass or shredded paper. Mix the candy and filler together with your hands. (If you can't find a specific kind of candy that's listed, just leave out the associated riddle.)

2. Choose a race area where the players can run safely. Divide the players into two teams, and have them line up in the order they want to race on one side of the race area. On the other side of the race area place the buckets across from their team.

3. Once the players are in position, read the first riddle (see following) to the first two players on each team. Once the riddle is read, they each race to their team's candy bucket, find the candy that is the answer to the riddle, and rush it back to their team.

4. If they chose the correct candy to answer the riddle, they go to the end of their team's line and the second riddle is read to the next player in line. If they chose the wrong candy, they must go back and try again. The race continues like this until one team completes all ten riddles.

5. The riddles are as follows:

- A happy nut? *Answer:* Almond Joy
- A small gift a bee might give you? *Answer:* Bit-O-Honey
- Something that occurs after a good joke? *Answer:* Snickers
- A sound you hope your bones never make? *Answer:* Crunch
- Could also be called a sour brain? *Answer:* Lemonhead
- The name of the galaxy we live in? *Answer:* Milky Way
- What do baseball pitchers stand on? *Answer:* Mounds
- Famous trio armed with swords? *Answer:* 3 Musketeers
- Another name for big fat lies? *Answer:* Whoppers
- Nothing? *Answer:* Zero

M&M Mouth

There's nothing more hilarious than watching someone's mouth become full of candy she can't eat!

What You Need

A large bowl of M&M's

How to Play

1. Have everyone sit in a circle, and place a big bowl of M&M's in the middle.

2. The first person closes their eyes, reaches into the bowl, and pulls out two M&M's. If the colors match, she can eat them; if they do not match, she has to put them in her mouth and hold them there, *without eating them*, until her turn comes around again.

3. Every player continues to play in this manner, making sure not to chew or swallow any of her candy. Once they draw a matching pair they can then eat all the candy in their mouth.

Chocolate Head

A fun and comical candy party game! Just make sure your friends have a towel over their shoulders to protect their clothes!

What You Need

Plastic shower caps   *Mini marshmallows*
Chocolate syrup   *Timer*

How to Play

1. Divide your friends into pairs. One girl in each pair puts a shower cap over her hair. Her partner then covers the top of the shower cap in chocolate syrup.

2. The partner then stands about 5 feet away with a bag or bowl of mini marshmallows. The object of the game is to throw mini marshmallows at the chocolate syrup–covered head and to get as many of them to stick as possible within a 2-minute timeframe.

3. When the time runs out, whoever has the most marshmallows wins!

Jellybean Mountain

In this messy game a single jellybean sits atop a mountain made of flour. You and your friends are challenged to scoop out the mountain without letting the jellybean drop.

What You Need

Flour

Cookie sheet (with a rim)

Jellybean

Spoon

How to Play

1. To play this messy party game, first create a mountain-like mound of flour. This is best done on a cookie sheet to make cleanup easier.

2. Flatten the peak of the flour mound a little, and gently place a jellybean on the top.

3. To play, you and your friends take turns removing a spoonful of flour from the flour mound. The goal is to try not to let the jellybean drop . . . but eventually, it will. The girl that is responsible for the drop must dive face-first into the flour to find and eat the jellybean—no hands allowed!

Candybar Race

Give every player a Hershey candy bar still in its wrapper. The object of the game is easy: Simply unwrap your candy bar and eat it. The catch is, you have to do it without using your hands! Good luck!

Biggest Bubble Contest

Pass out some bubble gum and see who can chew and blow the biggest bubble! Yep—easy, simple, and so much fun!

Activity

What's better than jewelry? Jewelry you can eat of course!

Candy Jewelry

This is a perfect icebreaker or activity to have ready for when friends first arrive, or to do while watching a movie.

What You Need

Large clean needles

Fishing line

Scissors

Variety of candy, such as Life Savers, licorice, gummy candy of all kinds, Tootsie Rolls, and so on

Set up a variety of bowls filled with different candy that can be put on string to create edible jewelry. Let your guests show off their creativity, and create some fun partywear at the same time. You can use needles to string solid gummy candies, or simply string ring-shaped candy through the hole.

Candy-to-Go Favors

If you're having a candy sleepover, of course the obvious party favor for you to give your friends is (surprise!) candy. Consider filling a favor bag with candies that symbolize your friendship, and include a note about why you chose each type of candy. For example:

- Snickers: Because we have such a great time laughing together.
- Almond Joy: Because it is a joy to have you as a friend.
- Fun Dip: Because we have so much fun!
- Reese's Peanut Butter Cups: Because we go together like chocolate and peanut butter!
- Skittles: Because you have such a colorful personality.
- Sweet Tarts: Because having you as a friend is sweet!
- Now and Laters: Because I want to be your friend now, later, and forever!
- Life Savers: Because when life gets hard, we always have each other.

Neon/Glow-in-the-Dark Sleepover

Light up the night with this enlightening party idea! Invite your friends to glow with you at your neon sleepover. Use black lights to make everything glow in the dark. Ask your friends to wear plain black or white T-shirts (best for neon glow fun).

Handmade Neon Invitations

Make a statement with an invite that seems to have its own inner glow! With just a few materials, you can create stunning invitations with a uniquely personal touch!

What You Need

Paint pens in your choice of neon colors

8" x 11" black card stock

Glow-in-the-dark stickers

How to Make

1. Fold your card stock in half.

2. On the outside of the invitation, use your paint pens and stickers to create a fun cover with the wording of your choice. An example would be, "You're Invited to Brianna's Totally Awesome Cool Glow-in-the-Dark Sleepover!"

3. On the inside, use the paint pens to write down all details of your party.

4. Use the pens and stickers to further decorate the invitations.

Digital Alternative

The great thing about creating invitations on the computer is that you only need to make one invitation, and then you can print out as many as you need. If you have a graphics program on your computer that you know how to use, create an invitation using neon graphics, lettering, and your choice of fonts. If you don't know how to use a graphics program but would prefer this option, you can ask a knowledgeable friend or adult to help you.

Illuminating Menu

For a neon party, food and drink items that will glow under a black light are a bright idea! Here are also some cool tips on how to set up and display nonglowing food to coordinate with the glow-in-the-dark theme. First of all, you'll need a black light set up over your buffet table for best effect. You can swap a regular light bulb in your ceiling light with a black-light bulb, or set up a table lamp with a black-light bulb on the table itself.

Glow Punch

How cool is a bowl of glowing punch? Setting up this punch bowl absolutely requires the supervision and participation of an adult. Dry ice is fun to use, but let a parent handle it. Never let it touch bare skin, don't try to eat it, don't directly breathe in the smoke/fog it creates, make sure the room is ventilated, and read up on how to transport and use it safely.

What You Need

A large punch bowl, with cups and ladle
Heavy insulated gloves
A tall plastic or metal cylinder container (A stainless steel coffee mug works great.)
Dry ice
Tonic water—warmed in microwave for about 20 seconds
Punch of your choice

How to Make

1. Place the cylinder in the middle of your punch bowl.
2. Fill cylinder about halfway with warm tonic water.
3. Fill the punch bowl with your choice of delicious punch.
4. Set a ladle and cups out for your friends to use to scoop out the punch.
5. When you are ready to make it glow, have an adult put on heavy insulated gloves (always use these when handling dry ice) and add a chunk of the dry ice into the cylinder. The dry ice will create a fun fog that will last about 5 minutes, and a glowing haze that will last for about 20 more minutes. If you want to see it again, ask the adult to add more ice and tonic.

Glow Gelatin

Everyone loves Jell-O, and your friends will love yours even more when it glows under your black light! The secret is the quinine found in the tonic water. Prepare to amaze them!

What You Need

2 cups tonic water

3-ounce packet of your favorite gelatin flavor

3 tablespoons sugar or sweetener

Gelatin mold or clear plastic cups

How to Make

1. Boil 1 cup of tonic water.

2. Pour boiled tonic water into a large bowl, and add the gelatin powder. Mix until it dissolves.

3. Mix in sugar, and 1 cup of cold tonic water.

4. Pour into your mold, or create individual servings by dividing the mixture among clear plastic cups.

5. Place in refrigerator for 3 hours, or until set.

Glowing Frosting for Cupcakes

Just like how the Jell-O glows, the way to make your cupcake frosting glow is with tonic water. Remember, you'll need a black light!

What You Need

7 cups confectioner's/icing sugar

1 cup vegetable shortening

1 teaspoon vanilla extract

11 tablespoons tonic water

Green neon food coloring

0.3-ounce package lime gelatin

Water

1 cup chilled tonic water

How to Make

1. In a large bowl, combine the confectioner's sugar, vegetable shortening, vanilla, and 5 tablespoons of tonic water together. Mix well.

2. Add 5–7 drops of neon green food coloring, or until the frosting has reached the desired color.

3. Frost your cupcakes. You can do this using a spoon or butter knife, but for a better presentation, put the frosting into a piping bag and pipe the frosting onto the cupcake in a swirl shape, bringing it to a peak in the center.

4. Place the cupcakes in the freezer for 1 hour to chill.

To Create the GLOW:

1. Empty gelatin mix into a bowl and add 1 cup of boiled water.

2. Add 6 tablespoons of cold tonic water into the bowl and stir well.

3. Place the gelatin mix in refrigerator to chill for 45 minutes to 1 hour. You do not want the gelatin to actually set; you only want it to be cold.

4. Dip just the frosted part of the cupcakes into the bowl of gelatin until it covers the frosting completely. Place the cupcakes back in the freezer for 3–4 minutes.

5. Repeat the last step six times for best results.

6. Place cupcakes under the black light to see them glow!

Other Ideas for Adding Glow to Your Buffet

• **Glow drink bucket:** Fill a large bucket or cooler halfway with ice and water. Activate a few glow sticks and put them at the bottom. Fill the cooler with drinks.

• **Glow drinking cups:** You will need clear party cups and colored party cups of the same size. In the bottom of the colored cups, place an activated glow bracelet. Now place the clear cup inside the colored cup, and fill with your favorite drink.

• **Glowing ice:** Fill an ice cube tray with a mixture that is half water and half tonic water. Freeze.

Decorations

Glow sticks, glow necklaces, and glow bracelets can be used very creatively when decorating for your glow party sleepover. Here are a few stellar ideas; what others can you come up with?

- **Glow Balloons:** Purchase a pack of neon-colored balloons and insert a glow necklace into each before blowing up. Hang from your ceiling for a fun effect.
- **Glow Bracelet Chain:** Connect glow bracelets to create a glowing chain. String across your party area the same way you would party streamers.
- **Create a Glowing Message** on your wall by connecting glow necklaces end to end and bending them to create letters. Use tape or sticky tack to connect them to your wall.
- **Glow Jars (adult help required).** Have an adult put on protective gloves and break open two or three glow sticks of different colors, then pour the liquid into a clear glass jar. Next, have them place two marbles in the jar and close the lid tightly. Now you will want to roll the marbles around inside the jar to coat the inside of the jar with the glowing liquid. Use for a centerpiece, or make a few using jars of different sizes and different-colored glow sticks and place them in different areas of your party room. You can also save this idea and use it as an activity for you and your friends to do at your sleepover. Provide a jar and enough glow sticks for each of your friends, and have an adult help all of you create your own.

Games

Regular games can become extraordinary when transformed into a glow-in-the-dark match! Here are a few classic game ideas with a glowing twist.

Ring Toss

This fun game is a neon-tastic spin on the game of ring toss.

What You Need

Glow stick
Candlestick holder (or use Play-Doh or clay)
Glow bracelets of different colors

How to Make

Activate the glow stick and place it in the candleholder (if you're using Play-Doh, make a ball, flatten it slightly, and push the glow stick into the top). Assign each of your friends a color and provide them 5 glow bracelets in that color. Count to three; on three, everyone must try to toss their glow bracelets onto the glow stick. You can take turns or go all at once. Whoever gets the most ringers win!

Glow Bowling

How many of your friends can get a strike?

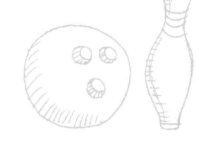

What You Need

10 empty 2-liter bottles
10 glow sticks
White rubber ball

How to Set Up and Play

1. Take any labels off of the bottles.

2. When you are ready to play, activate the glow sticks and place one in each bottle. Replace the lids on bottles.

3. Set up the bottles like bowling pins at a bowling alley: one in the front; behind that is a row of two; then a row of three; and finally, behind those, a row of four.

4. Standing about 10 feet away, take turns rolling the white ball to knock over the "pins." Keep score!

Bounce n' Glow

Challenge your friends to bounce the bouncy ball through the glowing hoop.

What You Need

3 glow necklaces
1 or 2 glow-in-the-dark bouncy balls

How to Set Up and Play

1. Create a giant ring about the size of a Hula-Hoop by connecting glow necklaces together, end to end.

2. Take turns trying to bounce glowing bouncy balls off the floor and into the hoop.

Glow Jump Rope

Connect glowing necklaces to form a long rope. Have a friend on each end turn the rope as everyone takes turns jumping. Make sure to switch places with the friends turning the rope so they get a turn to jump, too.

Activities

Here are a few activities to glow off, I mean show off to your friends.

Art Gallery

Create stunning works of glowing art in this radiant activity.

What You Need

Sheets of black poster board (one for each guest)
Black light
Liquid laundry detergent with whiteners (such as Tide)
Cups or bowls
Paintbrushes

What to Do

Hang the sheets of black posterboard along your walls. Set up a black light above the posterboard sheets. Provide cups or bowls of liquid detergent along with paintbrushes to your friends, and let them paint on the black posterboards. Laundry detergent with whiteners really glows! Just make sure that the cups or bowls you're using to hold it can't be confused in any way with your real drinking cups; you don't want any of your guests to accidentally drink it. You can mark the cups or bowls with masking tape, for example.

Glowing Bubbles

This is definitely an outdoor activity! Mix glow-in-the-dark washable paint with bubble solution to create awesome glowing bubbles. Don't try this indoors, or you'll get glow paint all over your walls and furniture. (This may sound cool to you. It probably will not to your parents, right?) Provide all of your friends with their own set of wands and bubble solution.

Glow Makeovers

Purchase glow-in-the-dark makeup or neon face paint before the sleepover. You and your friends can have a blast painting each other's faces. When you are done, check out your art under the black light.

Glow-in-the-Dark T-shirt Favors

Did you know that highlighters glow under a black light? Tell all of your friends to bring a plain white cotton T-shirt to the sleepover, and provide a variety of different colored highlighters to decorate them with. Yellow, orange, and green highlighters glow the best. The T-shirts make a great keepsake, especially if you and your friends decorate and sign each other's T-shirts. (Make sure you let your friends know that they'll be drawing on the T-shirts ahead of time, so they don't end up bringing a shirt they can't draw on.)

Chapter 13

Diary

All about Me Sleepover

What better way to celebrate the unique and adorable person you are than to have a sleepover that is all about you? Everyone should take some time and appreciate herself. After all, who is better than you? With this party theme, it's totally acceptable to adore yourself, and have your friends join in the fun celebrating how awesome you are!

Personalized Invitations

There are a couple of ways to achieve an invitation that really
centers on you. You can use some of the online sites where
you just choose a template, upload a photo and some details,
and they will do the rest. Another creative option is to make
your own using some of the following guidelines.

What You Need

Printer with ink

*Printable paper/card stock of your desired color and design (This can be found at most
craft stores.)*

A favorite photo (just one; this will help to keep the invite from being too busy to the eye)

Hole punch

Twine or ribbon

Scissors

How to Make

1. Begin by changing the document settings on the computer to Landscape (the default is usually
Portrait).

2. Upload your photo and crop it if necessary. Try to keep the photo to a size that will allow room
for your text around it.

3. Type in your sleepover details. Make
sure to proofread it! (A parent can be a
great help here.) Once you're sure it's okay,
print it out.

4. Lay the invitation on a flat surface and bring both sides in so that the ends meet in the middle. Crease the folds. The invitation will open up like double doors.

5. Use a hole punch to create a hole on each side of the center of the flaps.

6. Run the ribbon or twine through the holes and tie the invitation shut; now they are ready to distribute.

Me Menu

As you think about your favorite foods to serve at your sleepover, keep a couple of things in mind. Though the party is all about you, not everyone might be crazy about the foods you love. Here are some suggestions for a few simple yet imaginative foods that can be enjoyed by all.

Mini Me Pizzas

These little delights are great, because your friends can dress their individual pizzas to their own liking, and eat them fresh out of the oven.

What You Need

Muffin pans
Nonstick cooking spray
Several cans of flaky biscuit dough (Pillsbury makes a great one.)
Squeezable pizza sauce (If you are unable to find this, you can always put a bowl of pizza sauce out with spoons.)
Cheese, pepperoni, bacon, veggies (anything your friends might want to use)

1. Heat the oven to 375°F and spray the muffin tins with the cooking spray.

2. Have your friends each stretch out a biscuit, and press it into one of the muffin cups. Add sauce, toppings, and cheese.

3. Once everyone has made a couple of pizzas, bake them in the oven for 8–10 minutes. Your friends can even have a contest to see who made the tastiest pizza!

Pigs in a Blanket

This is a little turn on the classic hot dog recipe where taste is definitely at the wheel. The sauce is an added favorite that will have your friends coming back for seconds.

What You Need

Pack of beef cocktail wieners
2 cans roll-out croissants
½ cup ketchup

Curry powder, to taste
Cookie sheet

1. Heat oven to the temperature recommended on the croissant can. Roll out the croissants and separate, trimming each one in half.

2. Roll each of the cocktail wieners in a half-croissant and place on the cookie sheet. Bake for the time instructed on the can.

3. While the pigs are baking, prepare the dipping sauce. Place the ketchup in a small bowl and sprinkle with the curry powder. Add the curry powder a bit at a time and stir well, then taste it before adding more. Add curry powder, tasting as you go, until you reach your desired level of flavor. If you accidentally add too much curry powder, just add a bit more ketchup to offset the flavor.

4. When the pigs in blankets are finished baking, place them on a plate with the bowl of dip, and serve.

Raspberry Lemonade

If you would like to make this pink punch a little more posh, you can garnish it with lemon slices and raspberries.

What You Need

12 ounces frozen raspberry lemonade concentrate
3 cups water

2 cups ice cubes
¾ teaspoon lime juice
1 can lemon-lime soda

Put everything in a punch bowl or large pitcher and stir. Let stand for 10 minutes to get all the flavors combined, and then serve.

Fruity Dippers

The dip for this recipe is undeniably good. You may need to double the recipe depending on your group size.

What You Need

8 ounces cream cheese
1 (7-ounce) jar Marshmallow Fluff
Apples, bananas, pineapple, and strawberries (These fruits pair best with the dip, but you can use what you like.)
Toothpicks

In a medium bowl, mix together the cream cheese and the Marshmallow Fluff. Cut the bananas and apples into thick slices, trim the top off of the strawberries and chop the pineapple into chunks. Arrange the fruit around the bowl of dip, and stand back and watch it disappear.

Candy Bark

Begin by lining a cookie sheet with waxed paper. Use semi-sweet, dark, milk, or white chocolate as a base for your bark. Put the chocolate in a microwaveable container and heat in the microwave for 10-second intervals, making sure to stir after each interval. Continue heating and stirring until the chocolate is melted. Mix in any candy you would like to add to the chocolate. Some good suggestions are: candy-coated pieces (like M&M's or Reese's Pieces), chopped peanut butter cups, toffee pieces, or nuts. Once everything is combined, pour the mixture into the prepared pan, and put in the refrigerator to set. After around 30 minutes, take it out of the fridge and dump the chocolate onto the counter, keeping it covered by the wax paper. Hit the bark with a mallet or hammer to break up the pieces. Place on a tray or serving plate, and keep it refrigerated until you're ready to serve it.

Decorations

Getting ready for the sleepover that is all about you can be super easy if you use some of the following suggestions.

• Pick your favorite colors for the streamers, tableware and balloons. What could be better to create a super mood for your party than your favorite colors?

• You can blow up pictures of yourself from different points in your life. Use twine to make a "clothesline" from one side of the room to the next, and hang the pictures from it with clothespins.

• Purchase several small glass containers at a craft or dollar store. Fill them with water, and put a drop or two of food coloring inside of each one. Put your favorite flower in each container, and place them around the party room.

• Cut out circles from different colors of card stock or construction paper. Write one of your favorite sayings or quotes on each circle. Poke a hole in the top of each and run fishing line or ribbon through them, and hang the banner from the ceiling. Your friends will get to read them and learn a little more about what you like.

• Create a string of what looks like small lamps using a strand of lights and disposable cups (like Dixie cups). Puncture a small hole in the bottom of each cup and push the light through. The cup should stay on by itself. You can wrap each cup with strips of colored paper if you want to stick with your color scheme.

• Place Mason jars filled with your favorite candies all around the table and room. It will give color to the room, and also take care of some snacks as well.

Games

Get ready because these games are all about your friends and you getting to know each other better in one of the best ways possible . . . while having *fun*!

Spinning Secrets

If you are ready for a night of revealing secrets and getting some good giggle time in, then this is your game to play.

What You Need

Empty glass bottle

A variety of condiments, sour, and salty foods (such as pickles, mustard, soy sauce, vinegar, etc.)

Plastic spoons

How to Play

1. Begin by setting out all of the foods and the spoons.

2. Get all of your friends to gather in a circle and take a seat on the floor. Put the glass bottle on its side in the middle of the circle.

3. Ask for a volunteer to start the game, or you can select someone. This person will go to the center of the circle and spin the bottle.

4. When the bottle stops spinning, the person that it's pointing to has to answer a question to be asked by the spinner. If the person refuses to answer, they must eat a spoonful of the food selected by the spinner as a penalty.

5. It is now their turn to spin the bottle. Keep track of who answers and who takes a penalty, because the person to answer the most questions without penalty wins the game.

The Mad Tapper

All you need for this game is places to hide, a timer, and a bunch of your friends. They will have a blast taking turns trying to find you in the dark.

How to Play

1. Select someone to be the mad tapper to begin the game. This person leaves the room, and those remaining in the room find places to hide. Everyone, except you, is considered a decoy. Everyone can hide under couch cushions, blankets, pillows, or wherever they like. You can also create fake decoys using pillows and blankets.

2. Once everyone has found a good spot, one person will flip the light off. The mad tapper re-enters the room with a mission to find you. You are in charge of the timer; you can start her time once she enters.

3. The mad tapper taps the first person she finds. When tapped, the person hiding responds in a disguised voice. The tapper then gets one chance to guess who that person is.

4. If the tapper guesses correctly they win a hint. Another of the decoys still in hiding must call out "Yoo-Hoo" to give the tapper a hint at their hiding spot. If there are no decoys left then you (it) must be the one to call out "Yoo-Hoo." Once you are tapped, stop the timer and write the time down. Now, another girl gets a chance to be the mad tapper. After everyone has a chance to play the mad tapper, the person to find you the fastest is the winner.

Fly on the Wall

This game shows just how well your friends know you! This game is simple, but takes a little bit of preparation before the sleepover begins.

What You Need

Paper
Pens

How to Play

1. Before the sleepover, you will need to come up with a list of questions to ask about yourself. The questions can range from simple, like "What is my favorite color" to harder ones, like "What was my most embarrassing moment ever?" You will need to come up with a minimum of ten questions so that there are opportunities for everyone to answer a couple of them correctly.

2. When it's time to play, give everyone a piece of paper and a pen. You will then read off each question, and they write down their answer.

3. Once all of the questions have been asked, everyone passes their paper to the left to be corrected.

4. Read off the correct answers while your friends are checking their neighbor's paper. The person with the most correct answers wins the game.

Picture This

Using their artistic skills—or lack thereof!—your friends are sure to get a kick out of this little game.

What You Need

Markers, colored pencils, or any drawing tool you prefer
Paper for each one of your friends

How to Play

1. Have your friends gather together. Each one will need a piece of paper and something to draw with.

2. Everyone will draw her best picture of you. They can dream up any scenario they please and draw it out.

3. Once everyone has finished her art, you or an assigned judge will review the completed art and decide who has completed the best portrayal of you. That person gets a small prize, and you get to keep all the great depictions of yourself through your friends' eyes.

Activities

This party is all about you, and these activities give your friends a chance to celebrate you and their friendship with you in a fun way.

Round Robin

In this group activity, you and your friends will write a silly story together . . . and you just happen to be the main character!

What You Need

Notebook

Pen

Published book of your choice (see following)

How to Play

1. In the notebook, write the first line from the book you chose.

2. The first person to go will use the first line to start a story about you! Set the timer for 2 minutes. Your friend has that long to write whatever she pleases. When the 2 minutes are up, she then passes the notebook to the person next to her.

3. Reading *only* the last line written, the next person will write for 2 minutes, continuing the story from that last line written by the previous person. When the time is up, she then passes the notebook to the person next to her.

4. The notebook makes its way around the room in this way until everyone has had a turn. The last person writes an ending in her 2 minutes.

5. Read your story aloud for everyone to enjoy.

Framed

This activity can also be used as a favor for your friends to take home.

What You Need

Digital camera and printer
Foam frames (available at craft stores or online)
Foam stickers
Markers

How to Make

1. Have your friends decorate their frames with the available supplies.

2. Get your friends to line up and take a photo with you, one by one.

3. Print the photos off during the sleepover and pass them out. Everyone can put their picture in her own frame. If there is no available printer, you can have them printed at a later date and hand them out when they are available.

Who Knew?

An activity like this will help you to see yourself through the eyes of your friends. It's also a great way to get your sleepover started.

What to Do

1. When sending out your invitations, make a request that your friends each bring something with them that reminds them of you. It can be a picture of a place, a certain perfume, a song, or anything that may have special meaning to them.

2. Once everyone has arrived, all of your friends can take turns showing off what they brought and explaining why the item reminds them of you. You can also take turns guessing why someone brought the item they chose.

Personal Favorite Favors

Your favors should definitely be a reflection of you and all that you like. Consider a favor bag with little samples of things that you love. Here are a few ideas that some girls have used, but of course your personal favorite favors will be as unique as you.

- Tattoos that wash off with soap and water are a fun favor that can be used the night of the sleepover (check out party stores and craft stores for a selection of temporary tattoos).
- Glitter lip gloss or your preferred flavored lip balm
- Notepad and pen sets (Your friends can use them to make note of all the fun things that transpire throughout the night!)
- Slap bracelets (If you hand out an assortment, your friends can trade if they like.)
- Candy necklaces
- Stick-on body jewelry
- Little compact mirrors (These can usually be found online in bulk or at your local dollar store.)
- Using inexpensive twine and beads, create an original bracelet for each of your friends to remember the sleepover by.
- Mini candles of your favorite scent (For some added pizzazz, tie a ribbon around the top and curl it.)
- Glow sticks and necklaces (These are fun to use at the sleepover.)
- Pour two to three servings of your favorite powdered drink mix (like hot cocoa, lemonade, cappuccino, or Kool-Aid) into a bag, and tie it shut with curling ribbon (you can include marshmallows with the cocoa, or crazy straws with the other drinks).
- Purchase several of the carnival-style round lollipops and a few sheets of blank round sticker sheets, then print a picture of yourself and a short message on each sticker, and stick one to the front of each lollipop.